C000247028

The
CONFIDENCE
Workbook

Adrian Tannock

Dedicated to the memory of Bernard and Anora.

Adrian Tannock is a therapist and author who specializes in helping people boost their confidence and improve their motivation. Adrian established a successful therapy practice in 2005, and works with people from all backgrounds – including students, professionals, celebrities and sports people. He especially enjoys working with athletes, and often coaches up-and-coming prospects from the worlds of boxing and tennis. He also supervises the work of other therapists.

Adrian is passionate about helping people and loves to write. This is his third book; he has previously written about insomnia and procrastination. He lives and works in Manchester, and is a keen amateur photographer.

Teach Yourself ®

The CONFIDENCE Workbook

Adrian Tannock

Hodder Education

338 Euston Road, London NW1 3BH.

Hodder Education is an Hachette UK company

First published in UK 2012 by Hodder Education

First published in US 2012 by The McGraw-Hill Companies, Inc

Copyright © 2012 Adrian Tannock

The moral rights of the author have been asserted

Database right Hodder Education (makers)

The *Teach Yourself* name is a registered trademark of Hachette UK.

All rights reserved. No part of this publication may be reproduced, stored in a retrieval system or transmitted in any form or by any means, electronic, mechanical, photocopying, recording or otherwise, without the prior permission in writing of Hodder Education, or as expressly permitted by law, or under terms agreed with the appropriate reprographic rights organization. Enquiries concerning reproduction outside the scope of the above should be sent to the Rights Department, Hodder Education, at the address above.

You must not circulate this book in any other binding or cover and you must impose this same condition on any acquirer.

British Library Cataloguing in Publication Data: a catalogue record for this title is available from the British Library.

Library of Congress Catalog Card Number: on file

10 9 8 7 6 5 4 3 2 1

The publisher has used its best endeavours to ensure that any website addresses referred to in this book are correct and active at the time of going to press. However, the publisher and the author have no responsibility for the websites and can make no guarantee that a site will remain live or that the content will remain relevant, decent or appropriate.

The publisher has made every effort to mark as such all words which it believes to be trademarks. The publisher should also like to make it clear that the presence of a word in the book, whether marked or unmarked, in no way affects its legal status as a trademark.

Every reasonable effort has been made by the publisher to trace the copyright holders of material in this book. Any errors or omissions should be notified in writing to the publisher, who will endeavour to rectify the situation for any reprints and future editions.

Hachette UK's policy is to use papers that are natural, renewable and recyclable products and made from wood grown in sustainable forests. The logging and manufacturing processes are expected to conform to the environmental regulations of the country of origin.

www.hoddereducation.co.uk

Cover image © raven – Fotolia

Typeset by Cenveo Publisher Services.

Printed and bound by CPI Group (UK) Ltd, Croydon, CR0 4YY

Contents

Acknowledgements

Thanks to Hannah Gray, Gareth Palmer and Sian Schofield for their support and encouragement while writing this book, and to Victoria Roddam for the opportunity.

Introduction

When we lack confidence, it is often *debilitating*. The doubt, the self-consciousness and the missed opportunities conspire to hold us back. Overcoming such difficulties can be challenging, but the rewards are clear – with confidence comes greater self-respect and personal freedom.

Stepping beyond our limitations is rarely a straightforward journey. Positive change depends on many factors: a person's character, their circumstances, and the extent of the challenges they face.

As an experienced therapist, I have helped many people transform their lives. I have learnt that people progress the most when they concentrate on taking things one step at a time.

This book has been written to help you improve your confidence, and it *works*... You will be introduced to tried and tested principles, strategies and techniques designed to change the way you do things. Practise the exercises thoroughly and you will make progress. All you need to do is keep an open mind.

So – good luck, and I hope you enjoy reading this book as much as I enjoyed writing it.

Adrian Tannock

1

How to use this workbook

In this chapter:
- ▶ *You will explore the true nature of confidence, dispelling some myths along the way.*
- ▶ *You will learn how to get the most from this workbook, and discover the key ingredient of a confident life.*
- ▶ *You will need: a pen, an A5 pad and an open mind!*

What does confidence mean to you? For some, it means feeling comfortable in their own skin: being able to stand out from the crowd and knowing their place in the world. For others, it means pushing boundaries: believing in their talents and abilities and feeling capable of anything.

How would *you* define confidence? Write a sentence or two in the space below, describing confidence in your own words:

Confidence is

_____

_____

_____

How did you get on? Let's compare it with the *Chambers Dictionary* definition.

Confidence (noun):

► Firm trust or belief (i.e. in someone or something)
► Self-assurance, self-belief (faith in one's own abilities or attributes)
► Assuredness, especially in the outcome of something

I would sum up confidence with the following statement:

► Confidence is a state, feeling or belief stemming from reliance, appreciation or certainty.

When you feel you can *rely* on something, you are confident in it. When you *appreciate* the abilities or qualities of someone, you are confident in them. When you are *certain* about something, you are confident in that certainty. So, confidence is a positive experience based on your perception at that time.

The question is – how do you get more of it?

→ Confidence and you

As we noted earlier, confidence is multifaceted; it affects us on different levels:

► The *cognitive* level: our thoughts, memories and beliefs.
► The *behavioural* level: what we say or do.
► The *affective* level: our feelings and emotions.
► The *physiological* level: changes in our body; e.g. heart rate or perspiration level.

How we think, how we feel, how we act, and even how our body behaves reflects our confidence at any given point. It impacts on everything we do:

- ► Confidence is the difference between retraining for a new career or remaining stuck in a dead-end job.
- ► Confidence is the difference between feeling positive at the start of the day or just getting through it.
- ► Confidence is the difference between feeling relaxed or feeling anxious at a party.
- ► Confidence increases your ability to think, feel, communicate and act in an effective way, *even under difficult circumstances*.

Confidence affects us in many ways, which is why so many misconceptions about it exist.

→ Some truths about confidence

Some people believe that confidence is something you are born with; that it's a special quality, available only to the few. *It's easy to be confident if you're Tom Cruise or David Beckham!* And it is true – being talented or popular makes it easier to be confident... However, even talented or good-looking people sometimes lack confidence. In this, they are no different from the rest of us.

If confidence is *solely* for the beautiful, why do people often grow in confidence as they age? Confidence can be learnt, it is not a special gift.

And confidence is *not* the same as arrogance. The difference between confidence and arrogance is simple: arrogance *compensates* for a lack of genuine confidence. Arrogant people strive to be right while confident people can accept being wrong. Arrogant people put others down, whereas confident people have no need to belittle others. When truly confident, there is no need for arrogance.

We can look at confident people and think, 'Everything must be so easy for them!' This is not the case. Confidence does not render us immune to failure or disappointment, nor does it make us perfect.

Still, a life lived with confidence is a life worth living. It galvanizes and energizes; with greater confidence comes a sense of self-reliance, even when challenged. Confident people appreciate their better qualities, and tend to be more relaxed and co-operative with others.

Confidence changes life for the better, and – it feels good!

→ The anatomy of confidence

There are three distinct – but interrelated – factors that contribute towards confidence: a healthy attitude towards yourself, self-efficacy and an optimistic outlook.

A HEALTHY ATTITUDE TOWARDS YOURSELF

Imagine somebody you love dearly. Although your relationship will have been through its ups and downs, you will still treat them with kindness and respect. Do you treat yourself in this way? Anything less and you're undermining your own confidence.

When our self-judgement is harsh and unfair, we learn to fear the judgement of others. Nothing could be more damaging; confidence means accepting yourself as an individual, living *your* values and treating yourself well. We will discuss this more in the chapters to come.

SELF-EFFICACY

Earlier, we defined confidence as stemming from *reliance*. Self-efficacy means feeling capable, and taking action when required.

People with low self-efficacy overestimate the challenges they face, causing stress and procrastination. Confident people tend to believe in their own abilities – they have more control and generally do well in life. Much of this workbook is designed to boost your self-efficacy.

To some extent, confidence should come from competence. Unless you are a competent brain surgeon, it would be best *not* to feel confident about performing brain surgery. Here, confidence would prove fatal (at least to the patient). As much of this workbook is focused on practical skills, your increased confidence will reflect a real-life improvement in your abilities.

OPTIMISM

When something goes wrong in life, is it seen as a temporary setback or 'just typical'? People who lack confidence tend to explain events in pessimistic terms.

'*I always struggle around people... Bad things always happen to me... I can't do anything right...*' These thoughts are problematic because they are personal, permanent and pervasive; there is no room for hope. This is known as *pessimistic thinking*, and it wrecks our ability to be confident. Much of our work together will focus on improving this.

A healthy attitude towards yourself, a sense of self-efficacy and an optimistic outlook – improve these aspects of your thinking, and confidence increases.

Exercise 1

YOUR CONFIDENT DAY

► This simple exercise takes 5–10 minutes.

► The aim is to imagine how different your confident life could be.

If you felt consistently confident, what changes would you see? In a moment, take some time to relax and daydream about the life you want for yourself. Consider:

→ Would you wear different clothing?

→ Would you change career?

→ How would you interact with people?

→ How would people treat you differently?

→ How would you respond to difficulty?

→ How would you spend your leisure time?

→ What change would you see in yourself?

Then, use the space below to describe a typical day in your new, confident life. Imagine being truly optimistic, enjoying a good relationship with yourself and holding a strong sense of self-efficacy. Start at the beginning: describe getting up in the morning, and take it from there. Aim to be comprehensive, right through until bedtime.

Finally, take an honest look at your life at the moment.

There is a difference, no doubt. And yet: *you have the ability to change, providing you persevere.* So – resolve to make a difference and you will work towards your confident life.

A typical day in my confident new life:

_____

_____

_____

_____

_____

_____

_____

_____

Refer back to this exercise often. By contrasting where you are with where you want to be, you will build motivation to keep going even when things are tough. Confidence changes everything. Think about this now – if you could change just one thing to begin with, where would *you* start?

→ Everything is practice...

According to famous footballer Pelé, success means *practice*.

Your confidence can improve, but only if you engage with the exercises in this workbook – reading passively will not help. Some exercises will suit you better than others, especially at first. Persevere with each one until it makes sense, even if you struggle to begin with. You will make quick progress if you push through and keep practising.

KEEP AN OPEN MIND

Avoid the temptation to skip past the exercises, thinking: 'That won't work...' Approach this workbook with an open mind. Be willing to test out new ideas, even if they seem unfamiliar. As a result, your confidence will benefit.

TAKE SMALL STEPS

This workbook will guide you through a *process* of learning. Instead of racing ahead, take your time with each chapter. Allow things to sink in before moving on. People learn best by taking small steps *repeatedly*. Race ahead, and you take too many steps just once – the very opposite of learning.

ACCEPT THE CHALLENGE

Improving confidence is never a straight line from A to B. There will be wrong-turns, backward steps, learning curves and frustrations ahead. Accept the challenge! By confronting your fears and weaknesses, you *will* become stronger. With this improved confidence, many aspects of your life will change. Opportunity lies ahead – you just need to push yourself a little.

LEARN FROM YOUR EXPERIENCE

As you work through this book, be *connected* to your experience. Aim to observe and understand it; feel like you're a part of it. When you have a noteworthy experience – good or bad – pull it apart and learn from it. Confidence is not random, and learning comes from understanding. Don't put things out of your mind.

Instead, consider your experiences with an analytical eye. What thoughts, feelings or behaviours contributed to your confidence (or lack of it)? Ask yourself, 'What went right? What went wrong? What can I improve in future?' View your experiences as experiments, and you'll make the most of this workbook.

IF YOU PERSIST, THEN FAILURE BECOMES FEEDBACK

It is difficult to be philosophical about our difficulties in life. Confidence is an emotional matter, and setbacks often weigh heavily. So again – look at things analytically, and then try something else. Your 'failures' are just part of the learning experience. Ask yourself, 'What can I learn from this?'

FINISH WHAT YOU HAVE STARTED

Simply purchasing this workbook is not enough; half-heartedly reading it through (with the best of intentions) and leaving it to one side will not help. You have a choice – don't be one of those people who glosses over the exercises. If *you* persevere with this book, taking things a step at a time, then your confidence will improve. Give yourself the best chance possible and *finish what you have started*.

CONFIDENCE IS AN ABILITY

Some people have the ability to perform under pressure, they communicate easily with others and know what they want in life. These people have the *ability* to be confident. Like any ability, confidence can be developed. Recognize this fact, and you are *free* to build your confidence and change your life.

To *really* improve your confidence, work through each chapter slowly. Avoid skipping ahead – each chapter builds on the last. Some exercises require you to make notes; read with your notepad and pen to hand. You will also need to make notes while out and about, so make sure your notepad is portable (or use an electronic equivalent – storing things in your mobile phone will do).

Let's put this into action. As people, we underestimate our capacity to learn – especially when struggling for confidence. As we get older, we can feel stuck in our ways, or that things will never change. It is as if our successes in life become overshadowed by our difficulties.

Exercise 2

LEARNING FROM LEARNING

▶ This simple exercise takes 5 minutes.

▶ The aim is to understand how you learn best.

Think about something you have learnt to do well; any skill or ability will do – it does not have to be of vital importance, just something you know you're good at:

➔ An element of your job you're particularly good at.

➔ An activity or hobby you enjoy doing well.

➔ A certain way you have with people.

➔ Something around the house – e.g. DIY or cooking.

And so on...

Next, think about how you learnt this ability or skill. Re-read the paragraphs (on learning) above, and relate that information to your own experience. How do you learn best?

Then, note three key points about learning in the space below. Draw on examples – so, perhaps your experience has taught you how to overcome obstacles, or how to think about things in a certain way. When it comes to learning, what *experiences* can you draw on?

Three things to remember about learning:

1 _____

_____

2 _____

_____

3 _____

_____

Growing in confidence means *learning*, which is something you already know how to do. That in itself should give you cause for optimism.

Where to next?

Let's review what you have learnt in this chapter.

► Confidence is a state, feeling or belief stemming from reliance, appreciation or certainty.

► Confidence affects the way you think, feel, act, and even how your body behaves; it impacts on everything you do.

► Confidence isn't exclusively for the talented or popular – it is not a special gift.

► Confidence and arrogance are not the same thing; arrogance compensates for a lack of true confidence.

► Confidence does not protect us from failure or frustration, but it opens up a world of opportunity. A life lived with confidence is a life worth living.

► Confidence can be learnt; it stems from a healthy attitude to yourself, self-efficacy and an optimistic outlook on life.

► Your confidence will grow as you engage with the exercises in this book. Keep an open mind, take small steps and complete the exercises. *Everything* is practice – this is the key ingredient to a confident life.

► You will need a notepad and pen (or electronic equivalent), ideally something portable, to get the most from this workbook.

In the next chapter, we will identify *when and where* you would like more confidence. You will discover a new tool for gathering information, and a new way of looking at your experiences. With this extra clarity, you will know precisely what needs to change for your confidence to improve.

Be more confident

→ What have I learnt from this chapter?

▶ _____

_____

_____

▶ _____

_____

_____

▶ _____

_____

_____

→ When can I practise these exercises?

▶ _____

_____

_____

▶ _____

_____

_____

▶ _____

_____

_____

② Confidence and you

Some people lack confidence only in certain situations. Others lack confidence in almost everything they do. Most of us fall somewhere in between the two.

Why did you buy this book (or why it was bought for you)? Perhaps a particular event illustrated your lack of confidence, or have these difficulties held you back for some time? Go through the following checklist, and tick anything that rings true for you. Add your own suggestions if required.

Exercise 3

'I WOULD LIKE TO HAVE THE CONFIDENCE TO...'

► This simple exercise takes one minute.

► The aim is to get a clear picture of your lack of confidence.

Work:

- ❑ Take phone calls in the office
- ❑ Attend meetings
- ❑ Get on with colleagues or clients
- ❑ Sit and eat with others
- ❑ Network confidently
- ❑ Apply for jobs
- ❑ Start or finish projects
- ❑ Ask for a pay rise
- ❑ Change my career
- ❑ Give presentations
- ❑ _____
- ❑ _____
- ❑ _____
- ❑ _____
- ❑ _____
- ❑ _____
- ❑ _____
- ❑ _____
- ❑ _____

Study or self-development:

- ❑ Enrol in college
- ❑ Attend lectures
- ❑ Pass a test or exam
- ❑ Ask or answer questions in class
- ❑ Start essays or assignments
- ❑ Pursue a hobby or pastime
- ❑ Attend group classes
- ❑ Learn a new skill
- ❑ Write a book
- ❑ _____
- ❑ _____
- ❑ _____
- ❑ _____
- ❑ _____
- ❑ _____
- ❑ _____
- ❑ _____
- ❑ _____

(Exercise 2 continued overleaf)

Health/Day to day:

- ☐ Improve my diet
- ☐ Start an exercise programme
- ☐ Stop smoking or drinking
- ☐ Be physically fitter
- ☐ Be relaxed in busy places
- ☐ Leave a bad situation
- ☐ Take criticism well
- ☐ Take more risks and pursue opportunities
- ☐ Confront old fears
- ☐ Feel good about the way I look
- ☐ Learn how to drive
- ☐ _____
- ☐ _____
- ☐ _____
- ☐ _____
- ☐ _____
- ☐ _____
- ☐ _____
- ☐ _____
- ☐ _____
- ☐ _____

Socially/Relationships and family:

- ☐ Be more assertive
- ☐ Speak in front of groups
- ☐ Make new friends
- ☐ Handle rejection
- ☐ Be comfortable with newcomers
- ☐ Take a compliment
- ☐ Stand out more with friends
- ☐ Talk on the phone to friends
- ☐ Say no to people
- ☐ Ask somebody out
- ☐ Start or end a relationship
- ☐ Handle insecurity or jealousy
- ☐ Meet my partner's friends and family
- ☐ Be a more effective parent
- ☐ _____
- ☐ _____
- ☐ _____
- ☐ _____
- ☐ _____
- ☐ _____

By listing the areas where you want more confidence, you have an idea of what needs to change. Over the next few weeks, add to this list if required. As the famous psychologist C.G. Jung wrote, 'We cannot change anything until we accept it.'

→ # Activating situations

As somebody who wants more confidence, you will find certain situations quite difficult. These are known as *activating situations*; they are the moments when we struggle to feel confident. Typically, activating situations fall into one (or more) of the following categories:

▶ **Social situations.** People with low confidence often find social situations challenging. Whether these situations are in work, with family and friends, or even just being outside of the home, problems with confidence are exacerbated by the presence of other people.

▶ **Task-based.** Confidence can be lost when confronted with certain tasks – particularly where our performance will be judged. At such times, our problems are caused by a lack of self-belief or optimism.

▶ **Automatic negative thinking.** Sometimes, negative thoughts pop into our minds *automatically*, robbing us of our confidence. Often, there will be an external cause – perhaps something subtle; at other times these thoughts just seem to appear, even when things are otherwise okay.

▶ **Anticipating or reflecting.** When we dread something, or beat ourselves up over an event in the past, confidence immediately evaporates. These situations, like automatic negative thoughts, are *internal* activating situations, destroying confidence from the inside.

What activating situations do you struggle with? Turn to the checklist at the beginning of this chapter and ask yourself, 'What examples do I have of this? When, where or with whom is this a problem?'

Consider the following example:

▶ 'I would like to have the confidence to *start essays on time*.'

Activating situations include:

▶ Being given assignments at university (task-based).

▶ Feeling really stupid in lectures (task-based; social).

▶ Avoiding opening text books (task-based; anticipating).

▶ Dwelling on last year's poor performance (reflecting).

These activating situations relate closely to the confidence problem – a lack of self-belief. Hence, they are mostly task-based in nature. Here is another example:

▶ 'I would like to have the confidence to *pursue opportunities that come my way*.'

Activating situations include:

▶ Panicking when my boss talks about promotion (anticipating).

▶ Lacking confidence when my friends ask me to go out (social; anticipating).

▶ Avoiding my self-employed friend because I know he wants to propose a business idea (anticipating).

▶ Ignoring my mobile when I don't know who the caller is (anticipating).

Here, the activating situations relate to *anticipation*; they might seem unrelated, but when you consider the dynamic at play (profound pessimism), there is a connection. Here is a final example:

▶ 'I would like to have the confidence to *feel good about how I look*.'

Activating situations include:

► Comparing myself to others and feeling bad about it (social).

► Resisting going to the gym because I feel too fat (social; anticipating).

► Calling myself fat and stupid all the time (automatic negative thinking).

► Travelling on trains because I feel in the way (social).

► Avoiding people's gaze when they walk past me (social).

► Hating my slim friends when we're out (social; reflecting).

This example includes *automatic negative thinking* and *social* situations; the confidence problem relates to a poor self-image, and is heightened by the presence of others.

Activating situations can be subtle. For the next week or two, look out for any situation you find difficult (or, more difficult than usual). As you can see, there is often a pattern – a clear relationship between our lack of confidence and the situations that worsen it.

Exercise 4

IDENTIFYING ACTIVATING SITUATIONS

► This simple exercise takes 5 minutes.

► The aim is to identify day-to-day activating situations that challenge your confidence.

1 Recall the times when, in recent weeks, you have lacked confidence. If required, use the checklist above to jog your memory. Ideally, focus on situations that keep cropping up. Write down five examples in the space below.

2 Then, note the type of activating situation it is (social; task-based; reflecting / anticipating; automatic negative thinking). Refer to the examples above if needed. Check if there is a pattern.

Activating situations from the past few weeks:

1 _____

_____

2 _____

_____

3 _____

_____

4 _____

_____

5 _____

_____

For the next week or two, pay close attention to your confidence. When you find things difficult, identify the reason; ask yourself, 'What just happened?'

What difficult experiences are you likely to face in the next week or two? Make a note below.

Over the next week or so, the following situations might challenge my confidence:

1 _____

_____

2 _____

_____

3 _____

_____

4 _____

_____

5 _____

_____

Learning to recognize activating situations *when they happen* means you can empower yourself in the moment. Let's expand on that now.

→ The ABCs of confidence

To be confident *in the moment*, you first need to gather information. By observing your response to activating situations, you can then learn to improve it.

In the 1950s, the influential psychologist Albert Ellis devised the ABC model to record our reactions to events in life. Using this model, you can capture your thoughts, feelings and behaviours as they happen. The model is really simple:

Activating situation – as we have just learnt, an activating situation *causes* a drop in confidence.

Belief – refers to the negative thoughts we have in *response* to the activating situation; for example, 'They don't like me', 'I can't do it', or *mental images* of things going wrong.

Consequences – the feelings, physiological changes and behaviours we experience as a result of our negative thoughts; for example, *anxious* feelings and a desire to *run away*.

To illustrate this further, here is an example.

CASE STUDY – ROBERT

Robert, a GP from Yorkshire, frequently attends networking events as part of his job. He finds them very stressful. Logically, Robert knows there is nothing to fear. However, he still becomes anxious, often finding himself loitering on the periphery.

Robert used the ABC model to observe his experience *in detail*. He recorded his thoughts, feelings and behaviours at three different times: thinking about the networking event (anticipating), attending the event (social situation) and dwelling on it afterwards (reflecting).

Robert's ABC tables

This was Robert's *experience* while travelling to the event.

Activating situation:	Anticipating the networking event.
Belief:	I get images in my mind of people staring blankly at me. My voice in my head says 'They won't like you', 'You won't find anyone to talk to', 'People will think you're weird' (and similar negative thoughts). I see a picture of myself standing on my own, while everyone else is happily chatting in groups.
Consequences:	As I think these thoughts, I get a strong feeling of fear and my heart rate increases. I don't want to go.

When Robert thinks about attending the event he gets upsetting visual thoughts. He hears his inner voice stating, 'They won't like you' and pictures himself standing alone. These thoughts lead to anxiety – it is no surprise that Robert's confidence suffers.

Next, Robert observed his experience at the event itself. (Wanting to be discreet, Robert used his phone to text himself observations when he could, and remembered the details later.)

Activating situation:	Walking into the room and seeing people standing together in groups.
Belief:	Strong thoughts in my head: 'What am I doing here? Let's just go'. Mental pictures of leaving, with my voice telling me: 'I don't need to be here... This will be a disaster'. I then had a strong picture in my mind of other people just walking away from me, leaving me humiliated and alone.
Consequences:	Strong anxiety, I even felt myself panic a little. Breathing shallow, heart racing. Sweating on back. Very unconfident.
	I wanted to approach people but I completely resisted. My legs went heavy, and instead I just lurked, avoided people and moved towards the exit.

Robert's lack of confidence gave way to fear. Thoughts came thick and fast, and it wasn't easy to record the whole experience. After a while he could slow his thoughts down. He recorded five distinct thoughts, which is enough.

As a GP, Robert spends a lot of time talking to people. But these networking events are different, and our confidence changes with *context*. Robert is confident in work, but much less so in day-to-day life.

Finally, Robert recorded his ABCs after the networking event.

Activating situation:	Reflecting on the networking event afterwards.
Belief:	Memories of feeling uncomfortable at the event. A strong thought (my voice) telling me, 'I'm useless'. A weird sense that it is no wonder that people don't like me.
Consequences:	When I thought 'I'm useless', I got feelings of frustration and sadness. I want to go back and do it again – properly – but that thought just makes me anxious. It's so frustrating!

In Robert's ABC tables, the relationship between activating situation, negative thinking and difficult emotion (and behaviour) is clear. He understands that it is irrational, but that doesn't help – his confidence is still badly affected.

Given his career as a GP, Robert's low confidence might seem difficult to understand. However, low confidence affects us in different ways; most people will struggle for confidence at some stage in their lives. By recording his thoughts, feelings and behaviours, Robert knew precisely what needed to change.

→ Taking action

Now it's your turn. For the next few days, whenever a situation seems *difficult*, make a note and pay special attention to your thoughts as they happen. (If you can, record your feelings and behaviours as well – but concentrate on your thinking). Aim to do this as frequently as possible. For instance, earlier in this chapter you specified five potential activating situations – pay close attention at these times, but aim to complete the following exercise *whenever* you find things difficult. The more information you gather at this stage, the better.

Sometimes you might lose confidence for no apparent reason. When this happens, try to pinpoint the activating situation. They are often subtle – even walking past an attractive person or struggling with a task at work can have an impact. And remember, automatic negative thoughts are an activating situation in themselves. Perhaps you thought something negative to yourself without realizing?

If you lose confidence when *anticipating* or *reflecting* on things, observe this as well. People are often surprised to learn they are destroying their confidence from the inside.

Keep the checklist at the beginning of this chapter in mind. When you encounter (or even think about) these situations, your thoughts and feelings may change. Note them down, and if you get stuck, re-read Robert's case study to guide you. As you'll see, it is very straightforward.

Exercise 5

DETERMINING YOUR ABCS

▶ This exercise takes just a few minutes each time.

▶ The aim of the exercise it to record your response to activating situations.

▶ Carry this out several times over the next few days.

▶ Remember that automatic negative thoughts, reflecting and anticipating are activating situations as well.

1 For the next few days, carry your notebook with you (or use your phone) and pay close attention to your confidence.

2 Whenever you find something difficult, identify the activating situation behind your drop in confidence. Pay particular attention to situations that keep cropping up.

3 Aim to observe (and record) as many activating situations as you can, paying particular attention to your thoughts as they happen (also note your feelings and behaviours if possible). The more information you gather at this stage, the better.

4 If you cannot discreetly record your experience *in the moment*, remember the experience as best you can, and make notes as soon as possible.

5 If your thoughts come thick and fast, just breathe deeply and slow them down – this becomes easy with practice.

6 Look out for automatic negative thoughts, or moments of anticipation or reflection. Make notes when they happen.

7 After gathering information in your notebook, transfer it to the ABC tables below. This is a necessary step towards improving your confidence.

It takes practice to record thoughts in this way. Asking yourself the following questions can help (either in the moment or as you remember afterwards):

Activating situation:

▶ Why is this situation knocking my confidence?
▶ Is it the situation itself? A task I have to do? Is it the people involved?
▶ Am I destroying my confidence from the inside?

Belief:

▶ Am I getting any visual thoughts?
▶ Am I saying negative things to myself?
▶ Are bad memories flicking through my mind?
▶ Is there a negative running commentary in my mind?

Consequences:

▶ What feelings am I feeling:
  ▷ In my stomach?
  ▷ In my chest?
  ▷ In my jaw, face, and legs?
▶ What physiological changes are there (heart rate, sweating, etc.)?
▶ What do I feel like doing?
▶ What do I *actually* do?
▶ Do I want to avoid or escape from this situation?
▶ Do I want to give up?

Exercise 6

ABC TABLES

When you have gathered your experiences together, copy this information into the ABC tables below:

The situation you found difficult goes in the *activating situation* section.

Your thoughts (your inner voice, memories, visual imagery, etc.) go in the *belief* section.

Any feelings, physiological changes and behaviours go in the *consequences* section.

Activating situation:	
Belief:	
Consequences:	

Activating situation:	
Belief:	
Consequences:	

Activating situation:	
Belief:	
Consequences:	

Activating situation:	
Belief:	
Consequences:	

Activating situation:	
Belief	
Consequences	

This exercise is a key step – it <u>must</u> <u>not</u> be glossed over. After completing the five ABC tables above, you're ready to carry on. Otherwise, you may not have enough material to work with.

Where to next?

By identifying those areas in life where you'd like more confidence, you have taken your first step towards personal *freedom*. It is not easy to confront our limitations. You should feel pleased for making a start.

For the next few days, remember to make notes *whenever* you lose confidence (in the moment or after the event is fine). Pay special attention to your *thinking*. Then, write up your findings in the ABC tables above.

In the next chapter, you will discover how to think with confidence. In the immortal words of Bruce Lee, 'As you think, so shall you become'.

Be more confident

→ What have I learnt from this chapter?

▶ _____

_____

_____

▶ _____

_____

_____

▶ _____

_____

_____

→ When can I practise these exercises?

▶ _____

_____

_____

▶ _____

_____

_____

▶ _____

_____

_____

3 *Confident thinking*

In this chapter:

▶ *You will discover how poor confidence is reflected in our thoughts.*

▶ *You will learn how to think more confidently, how to recognize distorted thinking and how to change mental imagery.*

▶ *The exercises in this chapter are for daily use; the more you use them, the more your confidence will improve.*

In the previous chapter we learnt about activating situations and the ABC model. Activating situations cause negative thoughts, resulting in a loss of confidence. Controlling your thoughts will improve your confidence, even in difficult circumstances.

Some people think predominantly with words. Others think mostly with pictures, or with a combination of the two. So, there are two types of thoughts we are concerned with: your *inner voice* and *mental imagery*.

→ Your inner voice

Without speaking out loud, recite the first seven letters of the alphabet in your mind. This is your inner voice, and it does a lot of your thinking for you.

Exercise 7

FINDING YOUR INNER VOICE

▶ This exercise takes just a minute.

▶ The aim is to listen to your inner voice and notice its qualities.

▶ When attempting exercises such as these, relax and don't try too hard.

▶ Read through the steps first and familiarize yourself with the exercise.

Think to yourself, 'Where is my inner voice?' If necessary, think it several times, and take a moment to observe:

→ Does it seem to 'come' from the front of your imagination or the back?

→ Is it coming from the left or the right?

→ Is the voice loud or quiet?

→ Does the voice sound confident or timid?

Record your answers in the space below:

Direction: _____

Volume: _____

Mood: _____

There are no right or wrong answers to these questions – each imagination is unique. You should find it quite easy to *tune in* to your inner voice; repeat the exercise again and, if you get lost, begin by reciting the letters of the alphabet (without speaking).

Our minds are rarely still. Mostly, our thoughts are trivial – for example, '*What am I having for dinner tonight?*' Sometimes our thoughts have a profound impact. This is especially true when it comes to confidence.

When we lack confidence, our inner voice becomes our *inner critic*. Perhaps nothing destroys confidence more than a voice in our head telling us, '*You just cannot do it!*' or, '*Why did I say that? I'm such an idiot!*' Do these thoughts sound familiar?

→ The inner critic

Look back at the ABC tables from the previous chapter. In particular, pay attention to the 'belief' section. Were your thoughts confident or critical? Did they help your confidence or hinder it?

Exercise 8

FIND YOUR CONFIDENT INNER VOICE

▶ This exercise takes just a few moments.

▶ The aim is to notice your 'inner critic' and replace it with a confident way of thinking.

▶ Use this exercise frequently over the next few days.

▶ Read through the steps first and familiarize yourself with the exercise.

1 Refer to your ABC tables from the previous chapter. Look at the 'belief' section, and identify any negative thoughts.

2 Re-think these thoughts several times. As you do so, observe the quality of your inner voice and record your answers below:

→ Does the voice come from the front of your imagination or the back?

→ Does it come from the left or the right?

→ Is the voice loud or quiet?

→ Does the voice sound confident or timid? Kind or unfair? Strong or weak?

Direction: _____

Volume: _____

Mood: _____

3 Now, think the very opposite thought in your mind. So:

→ 'I can't do it,' becomes 'I can do it.'

→ 'I'm not confident enough,' becomes 'I am confident enough.'

→ 'They don't want to talk to me,' becomes 'They are interested in me.'

And so on...

4 Imagine how your voice sounds when really confident. (If necessary, pretend to be confident now.) Re-think those positive thoughts, using this confident voice in your mind:

→ Is your voice louder? Clearer? Stronger?

→ Does it come from a different location in your imagination?

→ What difference is there when you imagine speaking with confidence?

Repeat this step until your inner voice sounds really confident!

5 Where (in your imagination) did your inner critic come from? Front or back, left or right? Next, imagine your *confident inner voice* speaking to you from this same location in your mind. State the confident thoughts again, and notice the effect it has on your emotions.

It's really simple. If your inner critic (the source of your negative thinking) sounds like it comes from the left side of your mind, then have the confident inner voice come from the same location. As we learnt in the previous chapter, thoughts create emotional responses. Think confidently, and your emotions will change.

Spend a minute or so practising with this now, and find your confident inner voice.

Don't be fooled by the simplicity of this exercise, it is incredibly powerful and can make a huge difference. Use it frequently in the coming weeks, and your confidence will improve.

CHALLENGING THOUGHTS

Replacing your inner critic with your inner confident voice is a great first step. However, sometimes negative thoughts are stubborn. They need to be taken apart before you can dismiss them.

We often forget that our thoughts are just... thoughts. Instead, our view of life is limited by thoughts that have little basis or logic. This is how confidence is lost. Ask yourself: *is my thinking perfectly accurate, or have I been wrong occasionally?*

CASE STUDY – JAMIE'S STORY

Jamie, a music student from London, was becoming increasingly anxious before performances. A promising violinist, most of her life involved practice, performance and study. Jamie had spent the past year working with a *very* critical teacher. As a result, her confidence was suffering.

Each year the college held an end of term concert, and Jamie was asked to perform a solo recital. Certain she would fail, Jamie felt terrible beforehand, and throughout the performance her mind was full of negative thoughts, *'This is terrible. I'm making a fool of myself... it couldn't get any worse!'*

After the concert, Jamie was amazed to be congratulated for her performance, especially by her teacher who was ebullient in his praise...

The recital had been a success. She had made some mistakes (which in her mind had been disastrous), but in reality her performance was far better than she imagined. Sometimes our thoughts are *just* thoughts, and they are not always to be trusted.

→ Cognitive distortions

In the case study above, Jamie felt certain her performance was a disaster. '*It couldn't get any worse!*' This thought was inaccurate – a distorted reflection of reality. She had turned the performance into a catastrophe, even though it was going well.

Does this sound familiar? Thinking becomes distorted in many ways. Read through the list below, and identify the negative thinking styles familiar to you (leave the space for your own examples blank for now).

COMMON COGNITIVE DISTORTIONS

► **Black-and-white thinking.** Viewing situations in 'all or nothing' terms – usually deleting positive possibilities in favour of the negative.

► Examples: *I'm a total failure. I can't do anything right. I'll never get anywhere. I'm never confident.*

Your examples: _____

_____

_____

_____

_____

_____

▶ **Perfectionism.** Judging people, situations and experiences with unrealistic expectations. Failing to take into account a fundamental truth – nothing is ever perfect.

▶ Examples: *I should have finished first. Everyone must like me. I must please everyone. I must get it right first time. I shouldn't have messed that up.*

Your examples: _____

_____

_____

_____

_____

_____

▶ **Catastrophic thinking.** Blowing things out of proportion and imagining the worst possible outcome.

▶ Examples: *I made a terrible mistake, I'm bound to lose my job, my home, my family. I can't do it, it'll be a disaster. I couldn't think of anything worse.*

Your examples: _____

_____

_____

_____

_____

_____

▶ **Negative generalization.** Taking one negative event to mean everything is negative.

▶ Examples: *He let me down badly – you can't trust anyone. I had an argument at work, I'll never fit in anywhere. I failed that exam, I'm going to fail the course.*

Your examples: _____

_____

_____

_____

_____

_____

▶ **Disqualifying the positive.** Dwelling on negative aspects to the exclusion of the positive; dismissing the relevance of anything that contradicts the negative.

▶ Examples: *He's only saying that to be nice. I fluked it. Yes the presentation went okay, but I made a complete fool of myself at the beginning. I'm a fraud...*

Your examples: _____

_____

_____

_____

_____

_____

▶ **Mind reading.** Assuming you know what others are thinking, despite not knowing the facts.

▶ Examples: *I can tell he doesn't like me. They're all judging me for my weight. I can't say that I'll sound stupid!*

Your examples: _____

_____

_____

_____

_____

▶ **Self-blame.** Unnecessarily taking things personally or taking responsibility, often in harsh terms.

▶ Examples: *I'm an idiot, it's all my fault. They were talking in the presentation, I must be really boring. I've brought this on myself and I deserve it. What a stupid thing to say!*

Your examples: _____

_____

_____

_____

_____

When we lack confidence, our thoughts become distorted. Which of these unhelpful thinking styles do you recognize?

Exercise 9

IDENTIFYING COGNITIVE DISTORTIONS

▶ This exercise takes 5–10 minutes.

▶ The aim is to identify cognitive distortions from your ABC tables (see the previous chapter).

1 Go through the list of common cognitive distortions again, with your ABC tables to hand.

2 Match your negative thoughts (listed in the 'belief' section of your ABC tables) to the categories above. Use the space provided to write down your thoughts. You may write the same thought in several categories – they are not mutually exclusive.

3 What other negative thoughts do you regularly think? Write down examples in the appropriate category.

4 Review your examples – how do they make you feel? Can you see the connection between this distorted thinking and your confidence?

This exercise demonstrates the difference between our thinking and reality. As you progress through this workbook, pay a lot more attention to your thoughts – if you don't control them, they *will* control you.

Exercise 10

CHALLENGING NEGATIVE COGNITIONS

▶ This exercise takes just a few moments.

▶ The aim is to notice – and challenge – distorted thinking as it occurs.

▶ Use the exercise frequently over the next few days.

▶ This exercise takes a little practice, so be persistent.

► Read through the steps first and familiarize yourself with them.

1 In the previous exercise, you wrote down examples of distorted thinking. Look at those thoughts now, and re-think them in your mind.

2 As you re-think these thoughts, ask yourself the relevant question below, using your inner confident voice:

→ Is it really 'all or nothing'?

→ Nobody is perfect, why does this matter?

→ Is this really a catastrophe? In five years' time, will I still care (or even remember)?

→ Just because this went wrong, will everything always go wrong?

→ What positives am I missing here?

→ How do I know what this person is really thinking?

→ Is this really my fault? My responsibility?

→ How real are these thoughts? They are just thoughts, are they not?

→ What would I say to a good friend who said this?

→ How does this thought serve me?

And so on...

3 As you ask yourself these questions, try to be *objective*. How distorted is the thought? How does it serve you to keep thinking it?

Spend some time practising with this. Out of the listed questions, one or two will make a real difference. It takes effort to challenge such thoughts, but your confidence will directly benefit. The only power thoughts have is the power you give them.

→ Mental imagery

People think with pictures as well as words. These pictures can be bright, vivid and moving, and they can be dull, fleeting and still. Sometimes, mental images *seem real*; at other times they are detached and distant. Each imagination is unique, but most people benefit from controlling their visual thoughts.

So, how does mental imagery work?

Exercise 11

TUNING IN TO MENTAL IMAGERY

▶ This exercise takes less than a minute.

▶ The aim is to make a simple picture in your mind (visualization) and observe certain qualities.

▶ Don't think too hard about the visualization; exercises such as these work best when you relax into them.

▶ Read through the exercise first and familiarize yourself with the steps.

1 In a moment, close your eyes and imagine a red helium balloon rising into the sky. Then, answer the following questions:

→ Could you see the colour of the balloon (in your imagination)?

_____

_____

_____

→ Was the balloon moving?

_____

_____

_____

→ Which detail(s) stood out the most?

_____

_____

_____

2 Next, close your eyes and imagine standing outside of your front door. Take a moment to relax into it, and imagine unlocking and opening the door. Then answer the following questions:

→ Could you see the colour of the door?

_____

_____

_____

→ Was the door life-size, TV screen-size, or in between the two?

_____

_____

_____

→ Was the image focused or fuzzy?

_____

_____

_____

→ As you imagined opening the door, did the image move?

_____

_____

_____

→ Did you see yourself standing in front of the door, or were you just *there*?

_____

_____

_____

→ When you imagined opening your front door, what feelings did you feel (if any)?

_____

_____

_____

For some, their front door (in their imagination) will be fuzzy, black-and-white and grainy. For others, the image will be clear, bright and focused. Typically, bright, colourful images affect us more than fuzzy, dim images but, again, there is no right or wrong way to use your imagination.

Repeat step 2 of this exercise several times. Make it *feel* like coming home. You can do this by imagining the door to be bright, focused, and as if you were standing in front of it. Practise now, and see how you get on.

Now, refer to the ABC tables from Chapter 2. Did you record any visual thoughts? If so, think back to *how* those thoughts played through your mind. Let's try another exercise.

Exercise 12

CHANGING MENTAL IMAGERY

▶ This exercise takes just a few moments.

▶ The aim is to reduce the impact of negative mental imagery.

▶ With practice, you will soon master this technique.

▶ Read through the exercise first and familiarize yourself with the steps.

1 Look at the 'belief' section of your completed ABC tables. Is there any negative mental imagery? In a moment, close your eyes and run one of the negative images through your mind. Take a moment, and make it vivid. Then, answer the following questions:

→ Is the imagery colourful or black-and whte?

_____

_____

_____

→ Is it life-size, TV screen-size, or somewhere in between the two?

_____

_____

_____

→ Is it moving or still?

_____

_____

_____

→ Is it sharp or fuzzy?

_____

_____

_____

→ Is it bright or dull?

_____

_____

_____

→ Do you see yourself, or are you just *there*?

_____

_____

_____

2 When you run this image through your mind, what feelings do you feel?

_____

_____

_____

3 Next, change the imagery so:

→ It is less colourful.

→ It is smaller.

→ It is a still image.

→ It is fuzzy and dim.

→ It is in the third person, so you see yourself in your imagination.

When you run the negative image through your mind in this new *mode*, its impact should be negated – at least to an extent.

When you change your thoughts, you change your feelings. Like everything, it takes practice to change mental imagery. Visual thoughts can be fleeting and difficult to 'see'. It helps to *catch hold* of the image, and then patiently change it: remove the colour, shrink it in size, stop the motion, change the perspective, etc.

For some, there are no mental images as such. In such cases, don't aim to 'see' the image; instead use your imagination to *imagine* you are looking at something. You are still changing your thinking, just in a way which suits you. *Pretend* you can see it, and these techniques still work.

Later in this workbook, you will discover how powerful visualization techniques can be. For now, practise changing mental imagery when required. Have a go at this next exercise.

Exercise 13

CREATING POSITIVE IMAGERY

▶ This exercise takes just a few moments.

▶ The aim is to replace negative mental imagery with positive imagery when required.

▶ Use the exercise frequently over the next few days.

▶ With practice, you will soon master this technique.

▶ Read through the exercise first and familiarize yourself with the steps.

1 In a moment, close your eyes and re-think a negative mental image from the previous exercise. Note the 'location' of the image in your mind's eye: is it to the left or to the right; close to you, or further away; above or below the eye-line?

2 Again, change the image so it becomes black-and-white, smaller, still, fuzzy, third person, etc.

3 Next, imagine a *positive* version of this mental image:

→ If you imagined being nervous, replace it with an image of feeling confident and relaxed.

→ If you imagined avoiding something, replace it with an image of taking the opportunity.

→ If you imagined procrastinating, create an image of making a start.

→ If you imagined something going wrong, create an image of things going right.

And so on...

4 In your mind's eye, move the image so it sits in the same location as the previous negative image (see step 1).

5 Then, make the new mental image bright, colourful, focused and vivid. Suspend your disbelief and pretend it is really happening; relax and really get into it.

Again, this exercise should change your *state* – replacing negative feelings with confident ones. Later in this workbook we will use an in-depth version of this exercise. Practise with this simple version for now. Use it whenever negative mental imagery is a problem.

Over the next few days, be mindful of your confidence and aware of activating situations as they happen. Practise the cognitive techniques learnt in this chapter. It will be challenging at first, but you will quickly progress – these exercises are quite simple. Ideally, re-read this chapter several times before moving on.

Pay special attention to automatic negative thinking (thoughts that pop into your mind for no apparent reason). Left unchallenged, automatic negative thinking ruins confidence. Instead, use your new tools and your mindset will begin to change.

Exercise 14

THE ABCS OF CONFIDENT THINKING

▶ This exercise takes just a few minutes each time.

▶ The aim is to put what you've learnt so far into practice.

▶ Give yourself time to gel with the techniques; don't expect perfection!

▶ You will get better with practice.

▶ Writing up your experiences is an important step – remember to fill out the ABC tables below.

1 For the next few days, pay attention to your confidence. Notice when you find a situation difficult and remember to observe your thoughts. Make a note of them, if possible.

2 As you tune in to your thoughts, practise using the techniques learnt so far. As with anything new, this will challenge you; persevere and you'll make quick progress.

3 As soon as possible, use your notepad or phone to record your observations (about the activating situation, your thoughts and feelings, and the cognitive techniques attempted).

4 Aim to practise the techniques from this chapter in *at least* five real-world situations. Copy your notes from each experience into the ABC tables below.

→ Replace critical or pessimistic thoughts with positive affirmations, using your confident inner voice.

→ Challenge obvious cognitive distortions using the questions earlier in this chapter (see the exercise: challenging cognitive distortions).

→ Replace negative mental imagery as it crops up with positive visual thoughts.

5 The most important point to remember: it will be clumsy at first, with patchy results. These techniques are not difficult, and they will become second nature – but only if you stick with them.

Recording (and rewriting) your experiences is an important part of the learning process – resist any temptation to gloss over this step! Copy your findings into the tables below. And remember the advice in Chapter 1 – *take small steps, and allow things to sink in before moving on.*

To start you off, here is an example:

MY ABC TABLES – COGNITIVE EXERCISES

Activating situation:	*Meeting my boyfriend's sister (and her friends) for the first time.*
Belief:	*Anxious beforehand, picturing them not liking me. When we met, I was okay at first – she seemed really nice. Then her two friends arrived and I went quiet. Was thinking that they were judging me (I kept saying this to myself). I kept telling myself to say something, but then kept thinking that it sounded stupid.* *Had this really clear picture in my head of a girl from school for some reason!!*
Consequences:	*Tense, anxious, quiet, not myself. My boyfriend noticed I was quieter than usual but didn't say anything.*
Cognitive techniques used:	*I used the confident inner voice to tell myself that I didn't know what they (the two friends) were thinking. That helped me to relax a little.* *The technique to get rid of visual images worked well on the image of the girl from school.* *I didn't know what to think when I kept telling myself I shouldn't say anything; eventually I just told myself to 'stop worrying so much' (I think I used the confident voice) and then blurted something out to the group. At first I felt like an idiot but then everyone laughed (in a good way!) and I felt a lot better...*

The example above will help you decide which details are useful – you're aiming to record the *gist* of the experience, not each and every moment. (In this example you can see that her efforts were far from perfect, but also that she made good progress.)

Activating situation:	
Belief:	
Consequences:	
Cognitive techniques used:	

Activating situation:	
Belief:	
Consequences:	
Cognitive techniques used:	

Activating situation:	
Belief:	
Consequences:	
Cognitive techniques used:	

Activating situation:	
Belief:	
Consequences:	
Cognitive techniques used:	

Activating situation:	
Belief:	
Consequences:	
Cognitive techniques used:	

Write up your experiences in the tables above. Aim to complete *five* real-world experiences before moving on to Chapter 4.

Where to next?

You now have your homework for this chapter. Go through the exercises again and really get to grips with them; adapt them to *your* way of thinking. Then, apply them to real-life situations and complete the ABC records above. Use these techniques repeatedly, and they will soon become second nature.

In the next chapter, you will learn techniques to help with anxiety. In the words of author Anaïs Nin, 'Life shrinks or expands in proportion to one's courage'. Soon, you will discover this for yourself.

Be more confident

→ What have I learnt from this chapter?

▶ _____

_____

_____

▶ _____

_____

_____

_____

▶ _____

_____

_____

→ When can I practise these exercises?

▶ _____

_____

_____

▶ _____

_____

_____

▶ _____

_____

_____

4 Overcoming anxiety

In this chapter:
- ▶ *You will discover how low confidence leads to stress and anxiety.*
- ▶ *We will look at the importance of relaxation, both in the moment and on a permanent basis.*
- ▶ *You will learn mental and physical techniques designed to overcome fear.*

In the previous chapter you learnt how to think with confidence. However, confidence is not entirely dependent on our minds. The fleshy stuff around your brain (i.e. your body) has a part to play as well.

In this chapter, you will learn how to overcome stress and anxiety. Lacking confidence is stressful. In difficult situations, the 'fight or flight' response kicks in, and we struggle to maintain control. More on this in a moment.

The exercises in this chapter will teach you how to stay in control. With practice, you will handle difficult situations more easily – especially when you combine these techniques with the tools you have learnt so far.

→ What is anxiety?

Imagine a zebra grazing on the plains of Africa. Should the zebra see a lion, its fight or flight response will activate, and many physiological changes will occur: heart rate increases, blood vessels constrict, adrenaline is released, and the animal prepares to flee because it is afraid.

▶ The zebra *fears* being killed and eaten.
▶ This fear *motivates* the zebra to avoid that outcome.

For the zebra, this is a useful response.

Anxiety produces the same fearful responses, except with anxiety the threat is not real – it is imagined. In our example, the zebra would still exhibit all of the signs of fear despite being in no danger. As a result, the zebra would be unable to function even though the fear was *baseless*.

When you find a situation difficult, do you feel anxious? Most likely; for many people, confidence-damaging situations also contain an imagined threat:

▶ The perceived threat of failure.
▶ The perceived threat of humiliation.
▶ The perceived threat of rejection.
▶ The perceived threat of being trapped.
▶ The perceived threat of confirming one's own uselessness.

And so on...

As we learnt in the previous chapter, our thoughts are often distorted – life is rarely as bad as it seems *in our imagination*. Typically, the anxiety we feel is also baseless. Think about this for a moment. How much more confident would you be in any situation if you understood: **there is no lion?**

→ How to relax

The antidote to anxiety is relaxation. Relaxation won't make you instantly confident, but it represents a major step. We'll explore two exercises that will help: *the quick relax* and *progressive muscular relaxation*. These techniques should become part of your daily routine.

There should be no fear or guilt associated with this; with greater relaxation, your performance in life will generally improve. The following exercises are vital to building better confidence.

Exercise 15

THE QUICK RELAX

▶ This exercise takes just a few moments.

▶ The aim is to use slow breathing and affirmations to relax your physiology.

▶ Use this technique many times over the next few days, particularly in difficult situations.

1 Whenever you are tense, stressed or anxious, breathe in slowly through your nose, mentally counting to five as you do so.

2 Then, slowly exhale through your mouth, relaxing your shoulders as you breathe out.

3 Repeat this five times. When you exhale, relax your shoulders, jaw, back, stomach and feet. These areas of the body often carry tension.

4 As you exhale, you can think a confident, helpful thought, using your confident inner voice (see Chapter 3). You could use a positive affirmation relevant to your situation, or you could remind yourself, *'There is no lion...'*

This exercise takes just moments – use it many times each day. It combines well with the cognitive exercises from the previous chapter, so practise relaxing and changing your thoughts at the same time.

DAY-TO-DAY STRESS

People who lack confidence often feel persistent low-level fear. As a result, confidence becomes even more elusive and fearful habits are entrenched.

To combat this, you need to introduce regular relaxation into your life. What relaxing activities could you do, even just once a week, to combat stress? Hint: doing things for others *does not* count. Nor does watching TV – in fact some research suggests that watching too much TV makes us more stressed...

Relaxing activities include:
▶ Learning to draw or paint
▶ Going for a massage
▶ Going on a slow walk
▶ Yoga or Tai Chi
▶ Baking
▶ Cleaning (believe it or not!)
▶ Cycling
▶ Listening to your favourite music
▶ Taking a long, warm shower
▶ Reading fiction

This list is far from exhaustive. Remember: building relaxation into your weekly routine will improve performance in your day-to-day life. Put any irrational guilt to one side. What relaxing activities could you fit into your life?

1 _____

_____

2 _____

_____

3 _____

_____

Do something on this list once or twice per week. You might think, '*I don't have the time to relax. I can't afford it. I'd be wasting time!*' Relaxation isn't a luxury, it is a key ingredient to a confident and successful life.

Beyond engaging in a relaxing activity, the following exercise will also help – providing you use it regularly. It only takes 10 minutes; all you need is somewhere quiet and private where you can relax. Make your best effort to fit it into your life.

Exercise 16

PROGRESSIVE MUSCULAR RELAXATION

▶ This exercise takes around 10–15 minutes.

▶ The aim is to systematically relax the muscles in your body, relieving stress and anxiety.

▶ It is best to use this exercise once or twice per day.

▶ Your concentration will wax and wane as you go through it.

▶ After a little practice, you'll be able to remember the steps beforehand.

▶ ONLY use this exercise in a place where it safe to relax completely with your eyes closed; never use this exercise when your full concentration is required, e.g. driving, operating machinery, etc.

1 First, slow your breathing right down. Consciously defocus your eyes, so they go blurry and don't take anything in. For many, it helps to let their eyes close.

2 Focus on your shoulders: make sure they are not tense and hunched, but rather loose and relaxed. Give them a little shake, if you need to.

3 Now, focus on your scalp, and let it gently relax. Using a *slow calm voice*, say to yourself 'Now I relax my scalp. My scalp is becoming soft... and more relaxed... and let go...'

4 Now, focus on your forehead, and let it gently relax. Using a *slow calm voice*, say to yourself 'Now I relax my forehead. My forehead is becoming soft... and more relaxed... and let go...'

5 Now, focus on your eyelids, and let them gently relax. Using a *slow calm voice*, say to yourself 'Now I relax my eyelids. My eyelids are becoming soft... and more relaxed... and let go...'

6 Now, focus on your face, and let it gently relax. Using a *slow calm voice*, say to yourself 'Now I relax my face. My face is becoming soft... and more relaxed... and let go...'

7 Now, focus on your jaw, and let it gently relax. Using a *slow calm voice*, say to yourself 'Now I relax my

jaw. My jaw is becoming soft... and more relaxed... and let go...'

8 Now, focus on the back of your neck, and let it gently relax. Using a *slow calm voice*, say to yourself 'Now I relax the back of my neck. The back of my neck is becoming soft... and more relaxed... and let go...'

9 Now, focus on your shoulders, and let them gently relax. Using a *slow calm voice*, say to yourself 'Now I relax my shoulders. My shoulders are becoming soft... and more relaxed... and let go...'

10 Now, focus on your upper arms, and let them gently relax. Using a *slow calm voice*, say to yourself 'Now I relax my upper arms. My upper arms are becoming soft... and more relaxed... and let go...'

11 Now, focus on your lower arms, and let them gently relax. Using a *slow calm voice*, say to yourself 'Now I relax my lower arms. My lower arms are becoming soft... and more relaxed... and let go...'

12 Now, focus on your hands, and let them gently relax. Using a *slow calm voice*, say to yourself 'Now I relax my hands. My hands are becoming soft... and more relaxed... and let go...'

13 Now, focus on your chest muscles, and let them gently relax. Using a *slow calm voice*, say to yourself 'Now I relax my chest. My chest is becoming soft... and more relaxed... and let go...'

14 Now, focus on your upper back, and let it gently relax. Using a *slow calm voice*, say to yourself 'Now I relax my upper back. My upper back is becoming soft... and more relaxed... and let go...'

15 Now, focus on your lower back, and let it gently relax. Using a *slow calm voice*, say to yourself 'Now I relax my lower back. My lower back is becoming soft... and more relaxed... and let go...'

16 Now, focus on your stomach muscles, and let them gently relax. Using a *slow calm voice*, say to yourself 'Now I relax my stomach. My stomach is becoming soft... and more relaxed... and let go...'

17 Now, focus on your thigh muscles, and let them gently relax. Using a *slow calm voice*, say to yourself 'Now I relax my thighs. My thighs are becoming soft... and more relaxed... and let go...'

18 Now, focus on your calves, and let them gently relax. Using a *slow calm voice*, say to yourself 'Now I relax my calves. My calves are becoming soft... and more relaxed... and let go...'

19 Now, focus on your feet, and let them gently relax. Using a *slow calm voice*, say to yourself 'Now I relax my feet. My feet are becoming soft... and more relaxed... and let go...'

20 Now, focus on your mind, and the fuzzy space behind your eyelids, and imagine that your mind is become more and more fuzzy, and relaxed. Using a *slow calm voice*, say to yourself 'Now I relax my mind. My mind is becoming soft... and more relaxed... and let go...'

Repeat step 20, really slowly, for the next few moments. When you say to yourself, '...and let go...', let yourself relax even more. If it helps, say the relaxing affirmations in your imagination rather than speaking them out loud.

Remember: you cannot force yourself to relax! Do this exercise slowly, allowing it to unfold naturally. It is a simple process: *relax each part of your body, working downwards from your head, whilst affirming that you're becoming more relaxed.*

Use this exercise daily, and it will make a difference. Learning to relax is an important step towards greater confidence.

··

→ Anxiety-provoking thoughts

In the previous chapter you learnt how to recognize distorted thinking. To further eliminate anxiety, there are two more thought patterns to look out for: *inflexible thinking* and *pessimism*. Let's look at these in more detail.

INFLEXIBLE THINKING

Imagine two people attending an interview:

▶ One enters the interview room with the attitude, '*It's okay if I don't get this job*'.
▶ The other enters the interview room thinking, '*I absolutely must get this job or it'll be a disaster*'.

Of the two candidates, who is most likely to be relaxed (and therefore confident)?

Inflexible thinking creates anxiety. The more inflexible we are, the more anxious we become when life, inevitably, frustrates our desire for *control*. Typical controlling thoughts include:

▶ I must get this right.
▶ I cannot fail.
▶ I must make my boss / my partner's family / the new neighbour like me.
▶ I should not feel frustrated when I try this.

▶ I should be better at this.

▶ I shouldn't do that!

Any thoughts that contain the words 'should', 'should not', 'must', or 'must not' may create anxiety; these inflexible thoughts leads us to viewing things catastrophically, even when there is nothing to fear.

Sometimes the inflexible word (should, must, must not, etc.) is implied rather than stated. Can you spot the inflexibility in these thoughts?

▶ Think of something to say or they'll think I'm weird.

▶ I'll do that when I'm in the mood.

▶ I'll just agree with him.

Here they are in full:

▶ *I should* think of something to say, they'll think I'm weird.

▶ *I must not* force myself to do that now, I'll do it when I'm in the mood.

▶ *I must not* have conflict, I'll just agree with him.

Whenever you try to force yourself to do or be something (or not do or be something), you are thinking inflexibly. Think about those areas where you are currently lacking confidence. How does inflexible thinking contribute?

Exercise 17

IDENTIFYING INFLEXIBLE THINKING

▶ This exercise takes 5 minutes.

▶ The aim is to identify examples of distorted thinking.

1 Go through your ABC tables in Chapter 2, and pick out three inflexible thoughts from your notes. Remember: sometimes the inflexible word is inferred. Where required, rewrite the thought to include the inflexible imperative:

→ 'I'm so fat' becomes '*I must not* be so fat'.

→ 'I can't do it' becomes '*I must not* do it'.

→ 'I don't want to answer the phone' becomes '*I must not* answer the phone'

And so on... The key is to spot the *imperative*.

2 Use the space below to write down your answers (leave the spaces for a *rational alternative* blank, for now):

Examples of inflexible thinking:

→ Inflexible thought:

_____

_____

_____

→ Rational alternative:

_____

_____

_____

→ Inflexible thought:

_____

_____

➜ Rational alternative:

_____

_____

_____

➜ Inflexible thought:

_____

_____

_____

➜ Rational alternative:

_____

_____

_____

....

It is easy to change inflexible thinking; the difficult part is spotting it, especially as the inflexible imperative can be hidden. Pay attention to your thoughts whenever you feel anxious. Ask yourself: *in what way am I trying to control the situation?*

The following process changes controlling thinking.

Exercise 18

CHANGING INFLEXIBLE THINKING

▶ This exercise takes 5 minutes.

▶ The aim is to change inflexible thinking.

   1 Review your examples above. In the space for your rational alternative, rewrite the thought replacing 'I must', 'I must not', 'I should' or 'I should not' with '**I would prefer**'.

   2 Then, state something more realistic using the word '**but**'. Here are some examples:'

     → I *must not* annoy my boss', becomes '*I'd prefer* not to annoy my boss, *but* I will not get sacked if I do'.

     → '*I must* think of something to say', becomes '*I'd prefer* to think of something to say, *but* I can wait for the right moment'.

     → '*I must* not get this wrong', becomes '*I'd prefer* to get this right, *but* it will not be the end of the world if I make a mistake'.

Understand how, by using the words *prefer* and *but*, you are thinking with greater flexibility, and therefore less anxiety.

Learning to spot and challenge inflexible thinking is an excellent skill to develop. Such thinking can be subtle, often escaping detection. Pay attention to moments when you feel a) generally anxious, or b) as if something should or should not happen.

Approaching life with flexibility is a key skill. For some, mastering this one technique will dramatically improve their confidence.

PESSIMISTIC THINKING

Confidence requires a sense of optimism. Pessimistic thinking leads to stress, anxiety and reluctance. Pessimistic thoughts can be verbal or visual:

- ▶ I'll get it wrong.
- ▶ I can't do it.
- ▶ Nobody will like me.
- ▶ This will end in disaster.
- ▶ Why do I put myself through this?
- ▶ Visual images of things going wrong, usually in catastrophic ways...

Pessimistic thinking leads to *performance anxiety*, which is very damaging to confidence. The following cognitive distortions are usually to blame:

- ▶ **Self-blame.** Unnecessarily taking things personally or taking responsibility, often in harsh terms.
- ▶ **Negative generalization.** Taking one negative event to mean that everything is negative.
- ▶ **Catastrophic thinking.** Blowing things out of proportion and imagining the worst possible outcome.

At its worst, pessimistic thinking contains self-blame, negative generalization and catastrophic thinking *at the same time*. Such strong pessimism runs deeper than our thoughts, often reflecting negative and limiting core beliefs. We will focus on personal beliefs later in this book.

For now, challenge pessimistic thinking as you notice it. As with other cognitive techniques, changing pessimistic thoughts is easy, providing you spot them. Whenever you catch yourself predicting things will be a disaster (using your inner voice or by visualizing catastrophic outcomes), dismiss those thoughts using the techniques in Chapter 3.

Exercise 19

IDENTIFYING PESSIMISTIC THOUGHTS

▶ This exercise takes 5 minutes.

▶ The aim is to identify pessimistic thinking.

1 Go through your ABC tables from Chapter 2, and pick out three pessimistic thoughts (look for self-blame, negative generalization and catastrophic thinking).

2 Use the space below to write down your answers.

Examples of pessimistic thinking:

1 _____

_____

2 _____

_____

3 _____

_____

Were things really *as bad* as you imagined? Can you not, at the very least, practise and get better, or are things stuck this way forever?

COPING THOUGHTS

When pessimism gets the better of us, we need thoughts that help us *cope*. Here are some coping thoughts to use when pessimism or performance anxiety becomes a problem:

▶ Things don't just go wrong because it's me. That makes no sense.

▶ Nothing serious is going to happen.

▶ Whatever happens, it won't last forever.

▶ I can't predict the future: I don't know if this will be a disaster.

▶ It won't be as bad as I am making it out to be in my head.

▶ Anxiety won't hurt me, it just doesn't feel very good.

▶ Avoiding this won't solve anything – I'll push through it now.

When you find yourself thinking pessimistically, use these coping thoughts to help. If your pessimistic thoughts are visual in nature (images of things going wrong, etc.), refer to the visualization exercises in Chapter 3.

Text yourself some of these thoughts now and keep them on your phone. This way, you'll have them to hand when needed.

Exercise 20

THE ABCS OF ANXIETY

▶ This exercise takes just a few minutes each time.

▶ The aim is to use techniques from this chapter in everyday situations.

▶ The more you use these techniques, the better you will get with them.

▶ Writing about your experiences is an important part of the learning process – use the ABC tables below.

1 Over the next few days, be mindful of activating situations; pay attention when you feel your confidence worsen.

2 Pay particular attention to your anxiety, and use the techniques learnt so far. As with the cognitive techniques in the previous chapter, it might be difficult at first, but you will quickly improve with practice.

3 As soon as possible, use your notepad (or phone, or memorize) to make notes about the experience: the situation, the thoughts you had and anxiety you felt, and the techniques you tried.

4 Use the techniques from this chapter in *five* real-world activating situations. Copy your notes from each experience into the ABC tables below.

→ When you feel anxious, use the quick relax exercise.

→ Use the progressive muscular relaxation exercise at least once per day.

→ Challenge inflexible thinking whenever it arises.

→ Use coping thoughts (and other techniques – see Chapter 3) when thinking pessimistically.

→ Combine the cognitive techniques with the relaxation techniques where possible.

Ideally, use the *quick relax* exercise (and the exercises to deal with *inflexible* or *pessimistic* thinking) before you enter a difficult situation. Feel relaxed in anticipation of an event, and your confidence will noticeably improve.

As you progress with your 'homework', copy your findings into the tables below. Here is an example to start you off:

Example – anxiety exercises

Activating situation:	Standing in a long queue at the supermarket.
Belief:	Very anxious thoughts about needing to leave, wanting to run away. 'I just want to get out of here,' and 'Can we please leave?' running through my mind over and over.
Consequences:	Felt dizzy, my heart rate increased, and strong butterflies and nausea in my stomach. Chest felt tight. Was on the verge of quickly walking out of the supermarket (but I didn't want to make a scene).
Anxiety techniques used:	I used the quick relax exercise – that helped calm me down.
	I changed the thought 'I just want to get out of here' to 'I'd prefer to get out of here, but I will be okay' and that really helped.
	I used coping thoughts: 'nothing serious is going to happen' and that also helped.
	After a while I was still jumpy, but okay.

Here, combining physical and cognitive techniques proved successful. Anxiety is usually needless: *there is no lion*, remember?

MY ABC TABLES – ANXIETY EXERCISES

Activating situation:	
Belief:	
Consequences:	
Anxiety techniques used:	

Activating situation:	
Belief:	
Consequences:	
Anxiety techniques used:	

Activating situation:	
Belief:	
Consequences:	
Anxiety techniques used:	

Activating situation:	
Belief:	
Consequences:	
Anxiety techniques used:	

Activating situation:	
Belief:	
Consequences:	
Anxiety techniques used:	

Confidence is the *opposite* of fear; it should be clear why these exercises are so important. Aim to complete *five* real-world experiences before moving on to Chapter 5.

Where to next?

In this chapter, you have learnt how to overcome anxiety. Use these techniques frequently; go through each one several times before trying them in real life. Then, pay particular attention to activating situations as they crop up, and remember to apply your new skills.

Stay connected to your thoughts, especially when anxious or stressed. At this stage you are still learning, so keep practising. Also, incorporate the *progressive muscular relaxation* exercise into your day-to-day life.

Complete the five ABC tables in this chapter *and* the previous one before moving onto Chapter 5. There is no point racing ahead – give your new skills time to bed in.

Be more confident

→ **What have I learnt from this chapter?**

▶ _____

_____

_____

▶ _____

_____

_____

▶ _____

_____

_____

→ **When can I practise these exercises?**

▶ _____

_____

_____

▶ _____

_____

_____

▶ _____

_____

_____

5 Feeling confident

In this chapter:
- ▶ *You will learn how to feel confident.*
- ▶ *You will discover how negative feelings hold you back. Being confident means stepping beyond difficult emotions.*
- ▶ *Confidence is a state. By learning to change the feelings in your body, you will notice a significant improvement in your confidence in day-to-day life.*

In Chapter 1 we defined confidence as '*a state, feeling or belief stemming from reliance, appreciation or certainty*'. In this chapter, you will learn how to get into that state. To begin, let's look at negative emotions associated with a *lack* of confidence.

What does it feel like to lack confidence? The answer varies from person to person. However, people typically experience a combination of the following feelings and emotions:

- ▶ **Anxiety:** As discussed in the previous chapter, lacking confidence leads to stress and anxiety. As a result, we feel a need to *avoid* someone or something.

- ▶ **Braced resistance:** People who lack confidence often feel a *clenched* or *braced* feeling. When we don't want to do something, we dig our heels in.

- ▶ **Shyness:** When we lack *interpersonal confidence* we tend to go inside of ourselves, becoming overly fixated on our thoughts and feelings. At its strongest, shyness leads to feelings of profound embarrassment.

▶ **Pessimism:** As we discussed in Chapter 4, pessimism reflects deeper, problematic beliefs. As a result, we *feel* strong pessimistic feelings.

▶ **Frustration:** Lacking confidence can be debilitating. Frustration, and even anger, is often felt. These heightened emotions distort our thinking, making matters worse.

Strong emotional states make it difficult to think rationally or positively, and our lack of confidence persists. So, learning to overcome negative emotions is an important step.

CASE STUDY – PATRICK'S STORY

Patrick, a self-employed builder in his forties, was going through a rough time. His business was failing and his confidence was at an all-time low. Patrick had only ever worked in construction; it defined how he saw himself. As his business continued to fail, life became very difficult.

Each morning, Patrick would try to get himself moving, but he seemed unable to do so. He was caught in the grip of overwhelming negative emotions. Here's how it happened each morning.

Activating event: As Patrick arrived at his office each morning, he would see a stack of unopened, official-looking brown envelopes. The stack grew larger each day. This led to:

Negative thoughts: Looking at the unopened letters, Patrick would think, '*Oh God, what am I going to do? I'll never get out of this mess...*'

Negative emotions: These thoughts led to strong feelings of frustration, anxiety, pessimism and braced resistance. As a result, he avoided the letters and buried his head in the sand.

Further negative thoughts: As he felt these negative emotions, Patrick's thoughts became even less confident, '*Well that's it. I might as well pack it in now. On the scrapheap at 45... How will I be able to look people in the eye again?*'

Given the amount of fear, pessimism and resistance Patrick felt, it's obvious why he found it hard to take decisive action. How have negative emotions held you back in life?

→ Working with feelings

There is a strong link between our thoughts and feelings. Vividly *imagine* positive things and you will *feel* positive. The opposite is also true.

The following exercises use your imagination to change the feelings in your body. If you struggle at first, just relax and try to feel connected to your imagination. It's a bit like watching a film: suspend your disbelief and you'll be drawn in. Using the *quick relax* exercise (or the *progressive muscular relaxation* exercise) beforehand helps.

REMOVING NEGATIVE FEELINGS

People *can* change negative feelings. The following exercise might seem a bit abstract at first, but it is very easy when you understand what you're trying to achieve.

Exercise 21

SPINNING NEGATIVE FEELINGS

▶ This exercise takes 5 minutes; practise it often.

▶ The aim is to observe your feelings in a certain way and learn to change them.

▶ When you get the hang of this exercise, you'll realize it is very simple.

▶ Read through the steps first and familiarize yourself with them.

Part 1 – observing negative feelings

Spend a fair amount of time answering these questions. For some, this will be really easy; for others, it will take a little time.

1 In a moment, close your eyes and vividly imagine a confidence-sapping scenario. Make it vivid, bright, and so it feels as if you're there. Exaggerate things a little and suspend your disbelief, as if watching a film.

2 Imagine the scenario vividly enough, and you will start to feel *something* negative – especially in your stomach or chest. Ask yourself, '*What is happening in my body?*' Focus on the emotion you feel. Is it anxiety? Braced resistance? Pessimism? Frustration? Something else? Spend some time connecting with the emotion, and answer the following questions:

→ Where is the feeling in my body (stomach, chest, face, cheeks, shoulders, etc.)?

_____

_____

_____

→ How does the feeling move? Is it a rising feeling or a sinking feeling? Is it a tight knot, spinning clockwise or anticlockwise?

_____

_____

_____

→ Does the feeling move quickly or slowly?

_____

_____

_____

→ What texture does the feeling have? Smooth, fuzzy, rough, tingly, spiky, no texture?

_____

_____

_____

→ Is the feeling narrow, or wide? Is it hotter or colder than the rest of my body?

_____

_____

_____

→ How intense is the feeling, on a scale of 1–10? How much pressure does it generate, or is the feeling light?

_____

_____

_____

➜ If the feeling had a colour, what would it be (just guess!)

_____

_____

_____

Visualize the difficult scenario in your mind's eye several times to answer these questions. Remember, when you work with your imagination, the emotions will be weaker than in real life. Pay particular attention to your stomach and your chest.

Feelings loop back on themselves, creating a circuit. To work out how they move through your body, it helps to use your hands (as if you were showing somebody else). For example:

➜ Feelings can spin quickly in your stomach or chest (a tight feeling).

➜ They can move from your stomach, through your chest, and into your shoulders and throat (a rising feeling).

➜ They can move down from your chest and into your stomach (a sinking feeling).

➜ They can be in your torso, your legs, the top of your head, your shoulders or arms...

And so on...

Repeat Part 1 of this exercise several times, and really get to grips with your negative emotions.

Part 2 – spinning negative feelings

The second part of this exercise is straightforward. You're going to learn how to ease negative feelings away by spinning them backwards.

Imagine sitting in a bath, scooping up handfuls of water and creating waves. Then, imagine you could reach into negative feelings you feel and do the same thing, creating waves.

In Part 1 of this exercise, you observed how the feeling moved (up, down, spinning to the left or right, etc.) You are going to learn how to create waves in the feeling, so it *moves backwards*.

So, if your negative feeling moved from stomach to chest, you'd aim to push the feeling down – so it moves in the opposite direction – from your chest into your stomach.

▶ **It helps to link the movement with your breathing. Imagine creating waves of feelings (moving backwards) each time you exhale.**
▶ **For some, it helps to visualize a feather duster or waterfall pushing the feeling away.**
▶ **Many people find the bath metaphor (above) effective.**
▶ **Others may prefer to force the feeling to move in the opposite direction using their will.**

It does not matter, providing you find a method that works for you.

As well as moving the feeling backwards, aim to reduce its texture, width, speed and intensity.

➜ If the feeling is tingly, imagine it becoming softer.

→ If the feeling is wide, imagine it becoming narrower.

→ If you gave the feeling a red colour, imagine it becoming pink, and then white or grey.

This exercise is easier to experience than read about. Read through the steps first and familiarize yourself with them.

1 In a moment, close your eyes and *vividly* imagine the difficult scenario again. As before, observe the location, movement, texture, width and intensity of the feeling (as in Part 1 of the exercise).

2 Take a deep breath, and as you exhale, imagine brushing / easing / spinning the feeling backwards against itself. Continue to breathe deeply; each time you exhale, imagine the feeling moving powerfully against itself – so it moves in the opposite direction.

It takes just a little practice to use your imagination in this way. When you get the hang of it, you'll have a eureka! moment.

3 Continue spinning the feeling backwards while imagining the difficult scenario:

→ As you exhale, imagine the feeling moving powerfully backwards.

→ Imagine the feeling growing narrower and less intense.

→ What colour did you give the feeling? Make that colour weaker and fainter.

4 Continue with this for a minute or two. Naturally, your concentration will wax and wane. You'll need to refocus on the scenario, and bring the negative feeling back. After a while, one of two things will happen:

→ The negative feeling will lessen to the point of vanishing, even as you vividly imagine the difficult scenario.

→ The negative feeling will become its opposite, leading to a feeling of actual confidence.

Feelings naturally rise and fall in intensity. Practise changing feelings in all ways: texture, width, breadth and depth, speed, intensity and, especially, *direction*.

Several exercises in this workbook use this technique. Learning to be confident means learning to change the emotions in your body. Spend a good 10 minutes per day (over the next few days) practising.

Mastering this technique changes everything. Use it *whenever* you notice negative feelings in day-to-day life. Here is a similar exercise, designed to instil confident feelings.

Exercise 22

SPINNING CONFIDENT FEELINGS

▶ This exercise takes around 5 minutes; practise it often.

▶ The aim is to observe your feelings in a certain way and learn to change them.

► When you get the hang of this exercise, you'll realize it is really simple.

► Read through the steps first and familiarize yourself with them.

1 Most of us have felt confident at some point in our life. Can you remember such a time? If not, imagine how it would feel to be confident and in control.

2 In a moment, close your eyes and vividly imagine feeling confident. Imagine doing something confidently and feeling good. Spend a little time relaxing into it, and make it feel *real*.

3 Ask yourself, *'What's happening in my body?'* Answer the following questions:

→ Where is the location of the feeling in my body (stomach, chest, face, cheeks, shoulders, etc.)?

_____

_____

_____

→ How does the feeling move? Is it a rising feeling or a sinking feeling? Is it a tight knot, spinning clockwise or anticlockwise?

_____

_____

_____

→ Does the feeling move quickly or slowly?

_____

_____

_____

→ What texture does the feeling have? Smooth, fuzzy, rough, tingly, spiky, no texture?

_____

_____

_____

→ Is the feeling narrow, or wide? Is it hotter or colder than the rest of your body?

_____

_____

_____

→ How intense is the feeling, on a scale of 1–10? How much pressure does it generate, or is the feeling light?

_____

_____

_____

→ If the feeling had a colour, what colour would it be (just guess!)

_____

_____

_____

4 Next, imagine pushing the feeling so it spins strongly through your body *in the same direction*. Each time you inhale, attempt the following:

→ Imagine the feeling moving more quickly, and with greater depth and power.

→ Imagine the feeling growing wider, and more intense.

→ If the feeling is moving from your stomach to your chest (for example), push it up and beyond, into your shoulders and your face.

→ What colour did you give the feeling? Make that colour more vibrant and intense.

→ Make the feeling wider, more textured and stronger.

5 Spend a couple of minutes spinning the positive feeling around. Your concentration will wax and wane; if the feeling eases off, imagine being really confident and spin the positive feeling around your body once more.

6 Use your confident inner voice (see Chapter 3) to state to yourself, '*I am feeling more and more confident*'.

Spinning feelings is easy when you get to grips with it. Use these techniques often: weaken negative feelings and boost confident, positive feelings. This excellent tool will make a huge difference.

Exercise 23

THE ABCS OF SPINNING FEELINGS

▶ This exercise takes just a few minutes each time.

▶ The aim is to use techniques from this chapter in everyday situations.

▶ The more you use these techniques, the better you will get with them.

▶ Writing about your experiences is an important part of the learning process – use the ABC tables below.

1 By this point, you should find it easier to spot activating situations. Pay attention to your confidence levels, and especially the feelings in your body.

2 Whenever they arise, practise spinning negative feelings so they become weaker, and positive feelings so they become stronger. When you understand the technique, it is easy to use. Aim to apply it daily.

3 Make notes about *five* real-life situations where these techniques were used. Copy your notes into the ABC tables below.

→ When you feel negative feelings, spin those feelings backwards to negate them.

→ When you feel positive feelings, spin those feelings forwards to intensify them.

4 Where possible, combine the spinning techniques from this chapter with the cognitive and relaxation skills learnt previously.

5 Pay special attention to *anticipatory anxiety*; learn to physically relax and spin positive feelings quickly in such situations.

Before taking these techniques into the real world, go through these exercises several times and familiarize yourself with the technique. Then, as you progress with your 'homework', copy your findings into the tables below. There is an example to start you off.

Example – spinning feelings

Activating situation:	Manager's meeting at work
Belief:	Strong thoughts of 'I hate these meetings', 'I don't want to go', 'Everyone can tell, I'm so quiet...' The usual!
Consequences:	Anxious beforehand (anticipatory anxiety?). Feelings of resistance and pessimism.
Spinning techniques used:	I used the quick relax exercise, combined with the spinning feelings exercise, to reduce the pessimism. This worked really well before the meeting. In the meeting itself I tried to feel confident and spin it around, but it was hard to feel confident. I did feel a lot more relaxed though, and my mind was a lot quieter!

Here, spinning negative feelings (backwards) really made a difference – particularly to the anticipatory anxiety that was being felt. It was a challenge to feel positive in the meeting itself, but with practice that will get easier.

MY ABC TABLES – SPINNING FEELINGS EXERCISES

Examples of pessimistic thinking:

Activating situation:	
Belief:	
Consequences:	
Spinning techniques used:	

Activating situation:	
Belief:	
Consequences:	
Spinning techniques used:	

Activating situation:	
Belief:	
Consequences:	
Spinning techniques used:	

Activating situation:	
Belief:	
Consequences:	
Spinning techniques used:	

108

Activating situation:	
Belief:	
Consequences:	
Spinning techniques used:	

Learning to change your feelings is an incredibly powerful skill to have. Imagine feeling instantly at ease, even in difficult situations. Life would be so much easier.

So, practise these spinning exercises thoroughly. They really do work.

Where to next?

Let's pause for breath... So far you've learnt how to:

► Identify activating situations.

► Change your thinking.

► Overcome fear.

► Remove negative feelings.

► Create confident feelings.

Practise these techniques whenever the opportunity arises. Sometimes it will be easy, and sometimes difficult. This is the nature of learning – accept that as part of your experience, and you will grow as a result.

Take things a step at a time and consolidate what you have learnt. Soon, you will combine these techniques, challenging thoughts while relaxing and spinning feelings – all at the same time! Make that your goal before carrying on. There are five ABC tables above, but aim to get ten or more practice experiences under your belt before proceeding to the next chapter.

A word on feelings. People who lack confidence often feel disconnected from their body, except when fear strikes. Don't be discouraged. The exercises in this chapter will reconnect you with your emotions – you will be able to harness them in time.

In the next chapter, when you are ready, we will look at *confident action*. Until then, pause, reflect, and practise your new skills thoroughly.

Be more confident

→ What have I learnt from this chapter?

▶ _____

_____

_____

▶ _____

_____

_____

▶ _____

_____

_____

→ When can I practise these exercises?

▶ _____

_____

_____

▶ _____

_____

_____

▶ _____

_____

_____

6 Confident action

In this chapter:
- ► *You will learn how to take positive action.*
- ► *You will discover how negative programming holds you back, and learn new skills to build motivation and overcome procrastination.*
- ► *Use these techniques regularly, and you will replace negative behaviour with a new sense of optimism, determination and confidence.*

When we lack confidence, we struggle to take positive action. Unfortunately, nothing damages confidence more than our inability to act. You cannot think yourself confident alone; regular positive action is key.

For example, there are boxers who impress in the gym but disappoint in the ring. Overwhelmed by the occasion, they perform below par. In a way, they defeat themselves. Confidence doesn't just depend on action, confidence *is* action, especially when it counts.

Before we continue, let's review your progress so far. Read through the following list of exercises. Unless you can use the technique in day-to-day life, leave the box un-ticked. Be honest – there is no point in kidding yourself.

I can use the following techniques in day-to-day life:

Chapter 2:

❑ Easily identify activating situations as they happen.

❑ Pay attention to thoughts, feelings and behaviours as my confidence drops.

Chapter 3:

❑ Replace my inner critic with confident thoughts, using my confident inner voice.

❑ Identify and challenge distorted thinking.

❑ Reduce the power of negative mental imagery.

❑ Create positive mental imagery.

Chapter 4:

❑ Use the quick relax exercise.

❑ Use the progressive muscular relaxation exercise regularly.

❑ Challenge inflexible and pessimistic thinking.

Chapter 5:

❑ Identify negative feelings and use the spinning feelings technique.

❑ Use the spinning feelings technique on positive feelings.

As you can see, we have covered a lot of ground so far. Did you tick most of the boxes, or are the results a little patchy? If there are no gaps, well done; that is a great achievement at this stage. If you've not practised as much as you'd like, *don't panic*. This chapter is about getting things moving.

Tackling problems is not easy. The exercises in this workbook involve exposing yourself to challenging situations. Although this exposure builds confidence, the process can be stressful. So, at this stage, focus on what you *have* ticked. Even just one or two exercises means you made a start – already that sets you apart.

Let's step things up a gear. Even if you have done well so far, read through this chapter – there is always something to learn.

→ Negative programming

While reading this workbook, have you found yourself thinking, '*I'll do that later*'? Many of us put off challenges even when we know the rewards.

Procrastination is a complex matter – a whole book in itself. However, consider the following problems and tick anything that might apply to you.

► A lack of self-belief causing unwillingness, stress or anxiety. ❑

► A lack of optimism in your ability to create a good outcome. ❑

► A fear of failure or change. ❑

► A need to stay in your comfort zone overriding your desire to make things better. ❑

► A need for things to be perfect (and knowing they cannot be) causing inertia. ❑

► A belief that you don't deserve to overcome your difficulties. ❑

► A belief that, ultimately, somebody might do this for you. ❑

► A belief that if you start doing well, something bad will happen. ❑

► A belief that you can only carry out these exercises when you have time, energy or when conditions are perfect. ❑

▶ An intolerance of the discomfort caused by action. ❑

▶ Bad habits leading to impulsive avoidance. ❑

Each box is an example of *negative programming*. People who struggle with confidence often find such negative programming a problem. Confidence reflects *optimism, self-efficacy,* and *a healthy relationship with ourselves.* Acting decisively also requires these factors. There is a clear connection between lacking confidence and putting things off.

Limiting beliefs, bad habits, an intolerance of frustration or discomfort, and even our addiction to the familiar can be overcome. Negative programming is *emotional*. It feels real, particularly when our confidence is low, but it's neither rational nor helpful. Do you wish to be governed by limiting beliefs and bad habits, or would you rather set yourself free?

People learn by doing and reflecting. Repeated, positive action will increase your *ability* to be confident. That means taking action today. Habitually putting things off only holds you back. So, how can you change this?

UNDERSTANDING NEGATIVE PROGRAMMING

The first step towards overcoming negative programming is recognizing it. Go through the examples below. Ask yourself: *do I identify with this?* (There is space for your own notes, leave that blank for now):

▶ *Lacking self-belief* hinders progress, especially in challenging situations. We become unwilling and afraid, which makes anxiety worse. However, take small steps to begin, and your confidence will improve. As a result, the exercises become easier.

▶ *Solution:* learn to relax and overcome anxiety. Practise the exercises in Chapter 4 extensively, and apply those skills in *mildly* challenging situations. As you become more comfortable, start practising with the cognitive techniques (Chapter 3) and build up from there. Prove to yourself that you can do it.

▶ Steps to take:

1 Try mildly challenging situations. ❑

2 Use relaxation exercises to ease past anxiety. ❑

3 Replace negative thoughts with the following coping thoughts: ❑

   ▷ I can do this.
   ▷ Nothing bad is going to happen.
   ▷ Anxiety won't kill me.
   ▷ This is just an easy situation – I'll be fine.

▶ Where or when can I practise this?

1 _____

2 _____

▶ *Pessimism, a fear of failure or change, and even a desire to stay in your comfort zone* means you are thinking with the survival part of your brain. Understandable, but unnecessary – there is nothing to fear beyond your comfort zone. Consider this:

   ▶ You might become anxious at times, and you might have some difficult experiences. You are bound to make mistakes, but your confidence will improve with practice. That makes it all worthwhile, because one year from now any anxiety, frustration or embarrassment will be long forgotten.

   ▶ Avoid taking action, and your confidence will stay the same. One year from now, that will *not* be forgotten. You will still be stuck, and only because fear kept you so.

▶ *Solution:* same as above – learn to relax properly, and tackle the smaller exercises first. There is little to fear in taking small steps.

▶ Steps to take:

1 Try mildly challenging situations. ❏

2 Use relaxation exercises to ease past anxiety. ❏

3 Replace negative thoughts with the following coping thoughts: ❏
  ▶ I can do this.
  ▶ Nothing bad is going to happen.
  ▶ There is no failure providing I learn from the experience.
  ▶ With practice, I'll become more confident.

▶ Where or when can I practise this?

1 _____

2 _____

▶ *Perfectionism* is a subtle form of procrastination. A fear of the imperfect is actually a fear of 'not being good enough'. The result – we put things off for as long as we can.

▶ *Solution:* As the famous artist, Salvador Dali wrote, 'Have no fear of perfection, you'll never reach it.' As with the other solutions so far – relaxation helps to begin with, as will the 'spinning feelings' exercises in Chapter 5.

▶ Steps to take:

1 Try mildly challenging situations. ❏

2 Use relaxation exercises to ease past anxiety. ❏

3 Use the spinning feelings exercise to remove negative feelings. ❏

4 Replace negative thoughts with the following coping thoughts: ❏

 ▷ It doesn't have to be perfect.

 ▷ There is no such thing as perfect!

 ▷ Learning is better than putting things off.

▶ Where or when can I practise this?

1 _____

2 _____

▶ *Irrational beliefs* are problematic. If you only had *positive* beliefs, life would be straightforward – even in challenging circumstances. Unfortunately, the opposite is also true; negative beliefs make life needlessly difficult.

▶ *Solution:* you will discover how to change beliefs later in this workbook. For now, understand that beliefs are not real, they are just *ideas* held with conviction. Changing negative thoughts *in the moment* will help (see Chapter 3). Here are some facts:

 ▷ You do deserve to overcome your confidence problems, but nobody will do it for you.

 ▷ It makes no logical sense to think that, if you start doing well, something bad will happen.

 ▷ You *can* use this workbook even when tired, pushed for time, etc. Conditions will never be perfect. Commit to making a small start now.

▶ Steps to take:

1 Try mildly challenging situations. ❏

2 Use relaxation exercises to ease past anxiety. ❏

3 Use the spinning feelings exercise to remove negative feelings. ❏

4 Replace negative thoughts with the following coping thoughts: ❏

▷ I deserve to be confident.
  ▷ Only I can do this.
  ▷ I'm doing this for *me*.
  ▷ Nothing bad is going to happen.
  ▷ Now is the best time to do this.
  ▷ This is just an easy situation – I'll be fine.
► Where or when can I practise this?

1 _____

2 _____

► *Bad habits* and an *intolerance of discomfort* can be overcome, providing you anticipate the negative feelings in advance. Relax, and use the spinning feelings technique to ease difficult feelings away.

► *Solution:* learning to be confident, as with all learning, involves overcoming frustration. The antidote is relaxation. When bad habits stand in the way, practise with the exercises in Chapters 4 and 5 – they will make a difference. Prove to yourself that bad habits (and frustration) can be overcome.

► Steps to take:

1 Try mildly challenging situations. ❑

2 Use relaxation exercises to ease past anxiety. ❑

3 Use the spinning feelings exercise to remove negative feelings. ❑

4 Replace negative thoughts with the following coping thoughts: ❑
  ▷ I am learning to be confident.
  ▷ I'm doing this for *me*.
  ▷ Now is the best time to do this.
  ▷ Let's just make a start!

▶ Where or when can I practise this?

1 _____

2 _____

Now it's your turn. Reading helpful advice, no matter how insightful, will not make much of a difference. You know much of this already – it's mostly common sense. Let's try something different.

Exercise 24

BUILDING A MINI-ACTION PLAN

▶ This exercise takes 5–10 minutes.

▶ The aim is to identify opportunities to overcome negative programming.

1 Go through the list of negative programming again, and tick the box for any technique that will help in *your* particular circumstances:

→ Do you need to change or challenge negative thinking?

→ Do you need to change negative mental imagery?

→ Do you need to overcome anxiety?

→ Do you need to use the spinning technique on negative feelings?

→ Do you need to boost confident feelings?

2 Then, for each category, make a note of *two situations* where you can put these techniques into action. It could be at work, with friends, whilst shopping, in the home – wherever you can make a *special effort* to use the techniques learnt so far.

Even if you think that negative programming doesn't apply to you – still come up with two situations per category where you can practise. You should have a list of 10 situations in total.

3 Then, decide when you are going to make this happen. Aim to do two per day, and ideally start today (tomorrow at the latest). Be bold as you do so.

By completing this exercise, you are building a *mini-action plan*. Of course, plans are only useful if you put them into practice.

EXCUSING PROCRASTINATION

Knowing what to do *and actually doing it* are two different things. Even though you really want more confidence, a part of you would prefer to give up. Have you experienced reluctant thoughts and feelings so far? Read through this list of excuses – tick those you recognize:

▶ I'm too tired to do this now.   ❑
▶ I don't have enough time to make a start.   ❑
▶ I've got plenty of time, and I will do it – just not now.   ❑
▶ I don't have everything I need.   ❑
▶ I've got more important things to do first.   ❑
▶ Starting now won't make any difference.   ❑
▶ I don't really need to start that right now.   ❑

Which of these excuses do you recognize? These thoughts are persuasive because they sound so plausible when we think them. However, allow yourself to be persuaded by them, and your confidence will never improve. And as we discussed in Chapter 1, a confident life is worth living:

▶ **With confidence** we are more self-assured – even under difficult circumstances.

▶ **With confidence** we relax and co-operate with others.

▶ **With confidence** life tends to make more sense.

You too can achieve this, but only if you learn. Dismissing procrastination excuses is an important skill to master.

Using your confident inner voice (see Chapter 2), you can challenge these excuses when they arise. Confidently state, *'yes, but I need to do this now,'* and you will regain some control. The key is to believe your dismissal of the excuse; without belief, it will not get you far.

Other helpful affirmations to dismiss procrastination excuses include:

▶ I might be tired, but the truth is I can still do the exercises. Let's start now.

▶ I have enough time to start, even if I don't get it finished today. Let's start now.

▶ But I want to do this – I can use the spare time I have later. Let's start now.

▶ That's just an excuse – I don't need anything except my focus and determination. Let's start now.

▶ Putting this off is the only thing that will not make any difference. If I practise, I'll get better – let's start now.

▶ I don't need to start this now, but I want more confidence, so... let's start now!

Remember, use your *confident inner voice* for the full effect, and believe these challenges as you state them. End each thought with *'let's start now!'*

What affirmations can you come up with? Note them down in the space below.

Helpful affirmations to dismiss procrastination excuses:

_____

_____

_____

Dismiss procrastination excuses and you free yourself from irrational self-sabotage. Store the most useful affirmations on your phone for convenience, and use this technique whenever you struggle to get going.

→ Building motivation

Positive action requires desire and determination. For instance, consider the effort elite athletes put into their daily routines – it takes some doing. You don't need *that* level of determination, but you can benefit from some of their methods.

Many athletes routinely use visualization techniques to improve their performance, motivation, self-belief and preparation. As you read the following quotes, think about their career achievements and the effort it has taken:

- ▶ 'I just visualized and then executed my plan.' ~ Usain Bolt, Olympic sprint champion.
- ▶ 'Before every shot, I go to the movies.' ~ Jack Nicklaus, champion golfer.
- ▶ 'I have been visualizing myself every night for the past four years standing on the podium having the gold placed around my neck.' ~ Megan Quann, Olympic champion swimmer.
- ▶ 'I visualize myself making perfect runs with emphasis on technique... The more you work with this type of visualization, especially when you do it on a day-to-day

basis, you'll actually begin to feel your muscles contracting at the appropriate times.' Camille Duvall, world water-skiing champion.

These people have achieved much, and know what they're talking about. So, you're going to learn these techniques for yourself. Use the following exercise daily – ideally for the next week or so. As a result, you will accomplish more, and greater confidence will follow.

Exercise 25

BUILDING MOTIVATION

▶ This exercise takes 5 minutes.

▶ The aim is to focus on a task, build motivation and take decisive action.

▶ Use this exercise frequently, and especially when you feel reluctant to get going.

▶ Read through the exercise first and familiarize yourself with the steps.

1 Think of the positive action you'd like to take. In a moment, close your eyes and focus on the steps involved – imagine performing them as confidently as you can. Take your time, and make it feel *real*.

   → For example, if you want to confidently sit with others at lunchtime, you could imagine walking up to a table, asking if it's okay to sit down, and then taking your seat.

2 Repeat step 1, and tell yourself precisely what you're going to do – use your confident inner voice for full effect.

→ So, imagine your confident inner voice stating, 'I'll walk into the canteen, spot a table where I want to sit, walk over and ask if it's okay to sit down, and relax as I join in with the conversation'.

3 In the previous chapter we practised spinning feelings around your body. Think about how confident you want to be, and feel *determined* to act now. Spin the determined feelings around your body (as we practised) so they become stronger, faster, more visceral... Continue to spin the determined feelings and run through the steps in your mind's eye once more.

→ So, you imagine walking up to a table, etc. while stating your intent with your confident inner voice and spinning determined feelings around your body. Doing this all at once takes a little practice, naturally – but they are very simple techniques.

4 Say to yourself, in your confident inner voice, '*I am going to do this, now*'. Emphasize the 'now', and act *straight* away, dismissing any procrastination excuses if they arise.

This simple exercise links desire with *detail*. Follow these steps correctly, and you cannot help but want to act. Use this exercise repeatedly for the next week or so – really get to grips with it.

You can also use this exercise to *program* yourself to act at a later time. In this case, the fourth step would be to say, in your confident inner voice, '*I am going to do this at [a specific time]*'. Use this technique several times beforehand, and motivation will be much easier on the day.

Exercise 26

OVERCOMING NEGATIVE PROGRAMMING

▶ This exercise takes just a few minutes each time.

▶ The aim is to use the motivation techniques to undo negative programming.

▶ Writing about your experiences is an important part of the learning process – use the ABC tables below.

▶ You are now well-equipped to overcome negative programming: you have identified negative programming that holds you back.

▶ You know which techniques will help you beyond those limitations.

▶ You have identified ten opportunities to put those techniques into practice.

And, most importantly:

▶ **You now have techniques that will help you take action.**

Follow this process:

1 Review the exercise 'understanding negative programming' (at the start of this chapter). Here, you have a mini-action plan – a list of ten situations in which you can use the techniques you have learnt so far:

→ You might need to challenge negative thoughts (Chapter 3).

→ You might need to ease through anxiety (Chapter 4).

→ You might need to change your feelings (Chapter 5).

2 In a moment, close your eyes and vividly imagine one of these situations now. Just like an elite athlete, you are using mental rehearsal techniques. Make it clear in your mind: where you are, who you're with, the techniques you are using and how it will pan out (be optimistic).

3 Then, use the 'building motivation' exercise above; while building strong feelings of determination, talk yourself through the steps and affirm your commitment *to action*.

Ideally, complete the 'building motivation' exercise several times before taking action. If procrastination excuses pop into your mind – firmly dismiss them.

4 When the time comes, take action! Cross all ten situations off the list. Relax, and learn as you go.

5 As with previous exercises, use your notepad to write up your experience, and copy your findings into the ABC tables below.

There are five ABC tables below, but complete this process ten times before moving on to the next chapter. By that point, you really will be making progress. The benefits of this approach are twofold:

- ▶ All practice is helpful – you will improve your ability with the techniques learnt so far.
- ▶ You will undo the negative programming that has held you back.

Here is an example to start you off:

Activating situation:	*Taking the lift when others are there (instead of waiting).*
Belief:	*Strong thoughts: 'I can just wait for the next lift'.*
Consequences:	*Anxious, shy, tense and feeling really uncomfortable.*
Helpful techniques used:	*I used the quick relaxation exercise while waiting for the lift and that helped. Used the confident inner voice to tell myself, 'There is nothing to worry about – it's just a lift'. Used the spinning feelings technique to feel less anxious. That really helped.*

Example – overcoming negative programming

Here we can see that the mini-action plan was put into effect – with success.

MY ABC TABLES – ACTION EXERCISES

Activating situation:	
Belief:	
Consequences:	
Helpful techniques used:	

Activating situation:	
Belief:	
Consequences:	
Helpful techniques used:	

Activating situation:	
Belief:	
Consequences:	
Helpful techniques used:	

Activating situation:	
Belief:	
Consequences:	
Helpful techniques used:	

Activating situation:	
Belief:	
Consequences:	
Helpful techniques used:	

Remember – focus on the details, and take things one small step at a time.

Where to next?

In this chapter you have learnt the *theory* of overcoming procrastination. You are now better placed to take action and really get to grips with this workbook. Focus on the small steps, use the techniques in this chapter often, and step things up a gear.

Now is the time to tackle negative programming. You listed ten situations where you can practise your new skills – this should keep you busy for the next five days or so. Make good progress with this before racing too far ahead.

In the next chapter, we will look at negative programming from a different perspective – by letting go of the past.

Be more confident

→ What have I learnt from this chapter?

▶ _____

_____

_____

▶ _____

_____

_____

▶ _____

_____

_____

→ When can I practise these exercises?

▶ _____

_____

_____

▶ _____

_____

_____

▶ _____

_____

_____

7 Freedom from the past

There is a direct connection between childhood experience and adult confidence. As children, we constantly form beliefs about ourselves and the world. Many of these beliefs serve us well, whereas some beliefs are much less helpful – especially those formed in difficult moments.

We have all experienced difficulty in life; we can be misunderstood, treated unfairly, and feel isolated from family and friends. At such times, negative beliefs are created. Even if your childhood was generally positive, there will have been *some* difficult times. This chapter is about freeing yourself from the effect of such experiences.

Are your beliefs consistently positive? Absolutely not. Our beliefs are complex, and problems can arise. Inner confidence *is* a matter of personal belief, and children form beliefs easily. Let's discover how.

CASE STUDY – WILLIAM

Bill, a retired theatre nurse from Reading, was passionate about poetry. It had taken him years to allow others to read his work, and he was amazed that people liked it.

With some encouragement from friends, Bill joined a local poetry group and found it very enjoyable. He attracted quite a lot of attention – he was by far the oldest there, and was also very talented. Bill didn't mind; he had spent his whole life working with people. Except, when asked to recite his poetry for the group, Bill consistently refused.

Although he never dwelt on it, Bill had been bullied by a teacher at school, especially when reading to the class. He would stand, humiliated, in front of the class while the teacher mocked his efforts. However, this was many years ago and Bill had moved on.

And yet, something of his school years had stayed with him. The idea of reciting his poetry to the group terrified him, even though he knew there was nothing to fear. (In fact, when Bill thought about it, he had always avoided public speaking, to the point where he'd missed out on promotions because he thought, '*no, that's just not for me, really*'.)

Bill did not have vivid memories of his school days. To him, it was all ancient history. It took a while for him to accept that experiences some 50 years ago could still be affecting him. Especially given everything he had lived through as a medical professional.

Despite Bill's initial scepticism, he started to see that his teacher *had* taught him something: *standing in front of people will only make you feel bad*. This belief was firm in Bill's mind – he wasn't consciously aware of it, but it destroyed his confidence in certain situations.

Looking at Bill's story, we can see the following:

▶ Bill had a normal childhood, apart from the bullying.

▶ Through the bullying, Bill acquired the belief, '*standing in front of people leads to feeling bad*'. There is an emotional, childlike logic to this conclusion.

▶ The impact of this belief was being felt some 50 years later. Bill didn't ruminate on it – it was more of an unconscious understanding, but it *had* limited him.

▶ Being humiliated in front of a class and reciting poetry are not the same thing. However, our limiting beliefs are not logical, they are *generalizations*.

Understand that past difficult experiences can stay with us for many years; our thoughts, emotions, and behaviour are affected in ways that do not seem obvious at first.

Think about your own experiences for a moment. What negative, generalized beliefs did you acquire when you were young? What negative, emotional experiences may have created or reinforced those beliefs? Lacking confidence as an adult *does not* require a terrible childhood. However, your lack of confidence as an adult was (most likely) instilled when younger. Ask yourself these questions:

▶ Was I ever bullied at school?

▶ Did I always fit in?

▶ Did I have a teacher who made life difficult?

▶ Did I make friends easily or was I shy?

▶ Was I confident about my school work?

▶ What problems did I experience in the home?

▶ Were my parents (generally) supportive or critical?

▶ Did they take an interest in my life, or were they sometimes absent?

▶ As I went through my teenage years, did I lose confidence for any reason?

▶ How was my relationship with my body as I grew older?

And so on… These questions are not about blame – often mitigating circumstances play their part. Instead, this is about pinpointing: identifying those times when childhood confidence was lost.

It only takes a handful of bad experiences to create lasting negative beliefs. These experiences don't need to be awful or life changing – just everyday experiences that, for some reason, stay with us. Like Bill, you might have difficulty accepting that 'ancient history' could affect you to this day, but people who lack confidence as adults have generally experienced some difficulties at home, or in school, or elsewhere.

Perhaps, for you, this is not the case – there are no hard and fast rules. Let's look at limiting beliefs anyway; for many the following techniques will be of great benefit.

→ The past and negative belief

There are three negative beliefs that really damage confidence.

▶ I am not competent enough (which means something bad will happen).

▶ I am not worth enough (which means something bad will happen).

▶ Things always go wrong (which means something bad will happen).

Everyone acquires these beliefs to an extent. They don't sit at the forefront of our minds, instead they are unconsciously held, activating only in situations that challenge us (hence: *activating situations*).

Read the three negative beliefs (above) once more, and bring to mind any difficult experiences from your past:

- ▶ The times you were shouted at or criticized.
- ▶ The times when you got things wrong or were blamed unfairly.
- ▶ The times when friendships were broken.
- ▶ The times when you were embarrassed or hurt by others.
- ▶ The times when you were ignored or didn't get the attention you wanted.

It doesn't matter if, as an adult, you think these experiences were trivial – children learn differently. Consider the contexts where you struggle for confidence as an adult, and compare them with your childhood experiences:

- ▶ If you struggle to complete challenging tasks now, how did you get on as a child?
- ▶ If you're anxious around groups of people now, how did you get on as a child?
- ▶ If you struggle with relationships now, what were your key relationships (parents, friends) like as a child?

And so on...

Answering these questions will help you pinpoint where things changed. There will be a connection: the confidence problems you have as an adult will be reflected *somewhere* in the past.

Exercise 27

NOTING NEGATIVE EXPERIENCES

- ▶ This exercise takes around 10 minutes.

- ▶ The aim is to think back to when you were young, and identify experiences that damaged your confidence.

▶ The key is to relax and let your mind drift back – you cannot force yourself to remember anything.

> **Important – please note: do not write down or work with (in any way) any memory that you could describe as abusive. If you have experiences in your past that contain sexual, emotional or physical abuse, consider seeking the help of a qualified psychotherapist – a practitioner of EMDR (Eye Movement Desensitization and Reprocessing) would be especially useful.**

If your past contains this type of trauma, you *can* get help to overcome it. Many of the exercises in this book will help you, but abusive memories are beyond the scope of our work together.

1 Spend a bit of time thinking about the schools you went to and the houses you lived in as a child. Remember childhood friends, and your family relationships *back then*. Who did you spend the most time with? Where did the difficulties lie?

2 Use the space below to write down a brief description of *any* difficult memory that springs to mind. In school, with friends, and with parents or significant adults. Describe each memory in just a sentence or two.

3 Try not to judge these experiences as trivial, meaningless or ancient history. Instead, understand how they could be upsetting to a *child*.

4 There is also space to record any negative thoughts you associate with the experience. As you recall the memory, close your eyes and run it through your mind. Ask yourself, '*What does this mean about me?*' and write your answers down.

Before you start, here is one of Bill's examples:

My teacher, Mr. Wilson, shouted at me for getting an answer wrong.

He made me stand at the front of the class, and called me 'an idiotic

boy' or something like that. I had to stand there for around 30 minutes.

People were laughing at me when he wasn't looking.

Negative thoughts: That I am idiot. That other people enjoy

laughing at me. That it's bad to be 'on show' in front of others where

they can make fun of you. I hate Mr. Wilson!

Now it's your turn. Think back to negative, childhood experiences and quickly note them down. As you think back, you might feel a bit anxious or upset; that's just old emotion – when you've finished this exercise, do something that you enjoy: watch a favourite film, spend some time talking to a friend, etc.

My negative childhood memories include:

1_____

_____

_____

_____

_____

→ Negative thoughts: _____

_____

_____

_____

_____

2_____

_____

_____

_____

_____

➜Negative thoughts: _____

_____

_____

_____

_____

3_____

_____

_____

_____

_____

➜Negative thoughts: _____

_____

_____

_____

4_____

_____

_____

_____

_____

→ Negative thoughts: _____

_____

_____

_____

_____

5. _____

_____

_____

_____

_____

→ Negative thoughts: _____

_____

_____

_____

_____

Most people can come up with five difficult memories. For some, there will be many more. Over time, you may add to this list. If old, forgotten memories pop into your mind, use your notebook (or your phone) to make a note before you forget again.

Look at your list through the eyes of a child for a moment. Think back to being younger; remember being in that era, at that age... Can you understand how easily we form negative beliefs in childhood?

→ Changing old memories

The following exercise is designed to remove old limiting beliefs. It works on a principle of desensitization, and is incredibly effective.

To begin, select the *least troubling* memory on your list. There is no point jumping in at the deep end. Instead, let's take things a step at a time.

Exercise 28

VISUAL KINAESTHETIC DISSOCIATION (REWIND TECHNIQUE)

► This exercise takes 20–30 minutes.

► The aim is to render old memories emotionless via a process of desensitization.

► It involves repeatedly visualizing an old memory until you no longer feel anything about it.

► Read steps 1–11 through first, and get an idea of what you're aiming to do. It looks complicated, but is incredibly simple.

► The goal of the exercise is to reprocess a troubling memory so you can run it through your mind's eye:

  ▷ Consistently in black-and-white.
  ▷ Consistently from a third person viewpoint.
  ▷ At a fast pace.
  ▷ So it feels completely emotionless.

The exercise will unfold in three phases.

▶ At first, it will be difficult to achieve these aims. As you run the memory through your mind, it will flare into colour (instead of staying black-and-white). It will keep *pulling you in*, switching to the first person, instead of remaining in the third person... and so on.

▶ Quickly, it will get easier: only changing to first person or becoming colourful at emotional points, or when long forgotten (and often trivial) details are recalled. During this phase of the exercise, the memory will start to speed up.

▶ Finally, with repeated viewing, the memory will be easy to hold in the new black-and-white, third person mode. It will play quickly, and start to look like it's happening to somebody else.

So, for example, if you had a memory of being shouted at by a teacher, you might remember being sat in a classroom, and the teacher's angry face shouting at you (in the first person). There might be colour in the memory, and you might find it upsetting to remember.

After using this exercise, you will be able to picture the experience in the third person, so the teacher is shouting at a little version of yourself. It will be black-and-white, and you'll feel *no emotion*.

This exercise is easier to do than read about. If this is your first time using it, allow yourself time to learn how it works. It can be challenging at first. Perseverance is key.

1 Select a troubling memory from your list above. It could involve criticism, or rejection, or being misunderstood. It could be in the home, or at school, or with friends. Choose something that would trouble a child, even if you now feel it is trivial or in the past.

(If this is your first time using this exercise, aim to work with something relatively simple; even if you are experienced with this technique, never use it on memories of abuse or similarly traumatic experiences).

2 In a moment, close your eyes and remember everything that you can about the experience: where you were, who you were with, and the conflict or upset that occurred. It doesn't matter if you cannot remember much – significant detail will come to light as we work through it.

If you need to, 'fill in the gaps'. If you cannot remember exactly where you were, or who else was there – it does not matter. Make an approximation of the experience in your mind's eye, and the process will still work. Even a 'snippet' of a memory can be processed in this way.

3 Let yourself drift back – into that era, into your body at that age; wherever you were, imagine that space around you. Spend a bit of time *in the memory*, and gauge:

→ What feelings do you feel in your stomach and chest?

→ How strong are those feelings, on a scale of 1–10?

→ How did this upset you at the time? What conclusion did you draw?

For most people, spending 10 seconds relaxing into a memory will bring up *some* (but not all) of their emotional experience from that time.

4 Now, we're going to re-imagine the memory. Have you ever seen film footage from a CCTV camera? We want the same effect. Instead of *being there*, picture it in your mind from the third person point of view, so:

→ It is small, as if you're watching the event on a *small screen* in your mind.

→ It is black-and-white.

→ You can see yourself on the screen.

→ It is silent – or the sound is distant, muffled, and coming from the screen.

→ It plays slightly faster than in real life.

5 So, close your eyes and run the memory through your mind in this new mode – from the beginning to the end. Spend a bit of time building up how it looks from the third person point of view. Spend some time working out the order in which the memory unfolds, and aim to make it black-and-white and silent (even though this will be difficult at first).

Again – it is okay to fill in the gaps: you may not remember exactly who was there or where the event took place. It is okay to imagine the experience as it might have been.

6 In your mind's eye, once you have played the memory from start to finish – rewind it, so it plays backwards, from the end, back to the beginning. Again, spend some time working out the order as it plays backwards. This takes a bit of practice, but you will soon master it.

This part is really simple – in your imagination, work out how the memory will look in this CCTV mode as you rewind it (so people walk backwards, talk backwards, eat backwards, argue backwards, and so on...) Take a little time to work out the order as events play forwards, and then backwards.

7 Once you have played the scene forwards and backwards in your mind, repeat that a few times so you get the hang of how it looks in the CCTV mode as it plays. Then, play it forwards – and then backwards – five times in total. After those five times, open your eyes.

At first, this will be challenging:

▶ As you try to keep it small and black-and-white, it will become colourful.
▶ As you try to keep it in the third person, it will become first person (as if you were there).
▶ As you try to keep it on a screen in your mind, it will move towards you in your imagination.
▶ As you try to keep it silent, the sound will keep coming back.

So – just ease through this first stage and be patient. It normally takes around five minutes for a memory to change to the CCTV mode.

8 Did you play the memory forwards and backwards five times? Good, now close your eyes and play it forwards and backwards another five times.

Occasionally, as you play the memory forwards and backwards in your mind, you'll remember new details. When this happens, incorporate the details into the black-and-white visualization.

9 Did you play the memory through five times? Good, now – another five times...

10 At this point, repeat Step 9 again – playing the memory in the new black-and-white, third person mode, forwards and backwards five more times. Then, open and close your eyes and play it again – another five times.

11 As you repeatedly play the memory in your mind's eye (as described) – things will start to happen:

▶ **It will become much easier to keep the memory on the screen, in black-and-white, and in the third person.**

▶ **The memory will start to speed up – only the emotional parts may slow down, become colourful or switch to the first person.**

▶ **After a while, even the emotional parts of the memory will speed up, become black-and-white and easy to keep in the third person.**

▶ **After a while, the memory will start to look like you're watching somebody else on TV. In certain circumstances it may start to look humorous. This means the memory is mostly desensitized.**

This could take anywhere between 20 and 30 minutes, depending on the nature of the memory you're working with. So, close your eyes, relax, and complete the exercise up to this point. You'll know when the memory has been desensitized – *you'll feel completely detached from it.*

12 When the memory becomes easy to play quickly, in black-and-white, third person, etc., close your eyes again and put yourself right back in the experience. Remember it as vividly as you can:

→ Does it feel like *just an old memory*?

→ Do you feel unemotional about the experience?

→ Can you look at it dispassionately?

13 When you can answer these questions positively,
the memory has been completely desensitized. So –
keep playing the memory forwards and backwards
(in the new mode) until you feel completely detached
from it. Then, you will be ready to let go...

14 Aim to be thorough – keep going until you feel
completely detached.

It can take some time to desensitize memories. Although
laborious, this exercise is incredibly powerful. Change is
encouraged from within: target the right memories, and
your whole outlook on life will improve.

So – persevere with this technique, master it and make
it your own. Using this technique on *five* old, damaging
memories may take a couple of hours (spread over a
week or two), but it will make a huge difference to your
confidence.

ABOUT VISUALIZATION

Some people are more visually-minded than others. This
technique still works for the less visually-minded. Bear these
two things in mind:

▶ With practice, holding imagery in your mind's eye
becomes easier. As a result, you add a new way of
thinking to your mental toolbox.
▶ Even if you don't actually see the images (in your mind's
eye), this technique is still effective providing you 'just

know' what you are *imagining*. Knowing that a memory is playing through your imagination (in the CCTV mode) is as good as actually seeing it. Experiment with the process and adapt it to *your* way of thinking.

Ultimately, it is all about the feelings; if you feel less upset by past experiences, you have succeeded in your aim. *How* you achieve that is secondary.

Where to next?

In this chapter you have discovered the connection between past experience and belief. Experience is our greatest teacher, but if we are not careful, our experiences can limit us. This is especially true of difficult, childhood experiences.

For some, the exercises in this chapter will make a lot of sense. Certain key memories will stand out, of school-age bullying or critical parenting, for example. Desensitizing such memories weakens limiting, negative beliefs. Confidence improves *organically* as a result.

For others, this chapter will be challenging. The connection between experience and negative self-belief is not always clear. Memories are sometimes difficult to work with, and – compared with other exercises in this book – the rewind technique can seem a bit of a chore.

However, using this technique repeatedly for the next few weeks will make a huge difference. Whenever you are free of distraction (exception: closing your eyes and focusing on your imagination is not recommended in the bath!) aim to desensitize old memories. It works really well – so free up 20 minutes of your day and use it regularly. Your investment will pay off.

In the next chapter, we will look at limiting beliefs in more detail. Combine the techniques from this chapter and the next, and you have a process that changes everything. Greater confidence will follow...

Be more confident

→ What have I learnt from this chapter?

▶ _____
_____
_____

▶ _____
_____
_____

▶ _____
_____
_____

→ When can I practise these exercises?

▶ _____
_____
_____

▶ _____
_____
_____

▶ _____
_____
_____

8 Confident beliefs

In this chapter:
- ▶ *You will discover how limiting beliefs hold us back.*
- ▶ *You will understand how our beliefs are not reality, and learn a quick and effective technique to change them.*
- ▶ *Change the beliefs that hold you back, and you take your biggest step yet towards greater confidence.*

In the previous chapter, we referred to three core, limiting beliefs that fundamentally damage confidence:

- ▶ I am not competent enough (which means something bad will happen).
- ▶ I am not worth enough (which means something bad will happen).
- ▶ Things always go wrong (which means something bad will happen).

We aren't necessarily aware of our beliefs; instead they are woven through the fabric of our perception. Beliefs colour our view of ourselves, of the world around us, of the past *and* the future. They are our reality.

If our beliefs were sophisticated, nuanced and true – this would not be a problem. Unfortunately, many of our beliefs form when we are young, and are limited by *childhood logic*. As a result, our beliefs do not reflect the complexity of life.

Limiting beliefs are particularly evident in activation situations. At these times, our thoughts become distorted, as we saw in Chapter 3:

► A person wants to join in with a conversation in the office, but hesitates. They think:
  ▷ 'Nobody wants to hear what I've got to say,' (*I'm not worth enough*).
  ▷ 'That's stupid – you can't say that,' (*I'm not competent enough*).
  ▷ 'They'll laugh at me,' (*things always go wrong; I'm not worth enough*).

► Somebody wishes they could change jobs, but hesitates. They think:
  ▷ 'Who am I kidding? I should stick with what I know' (*I'm not competent enough*).
  ▷ 'I'm bound to mess it up and get sacked,' (*things always go wrong*).
  ▷ 'I should just settle down and be happy with my lot,' (*I'm not worth enough*).

► A nervous young man wants to approach an attractive girl at a party. He thinks:
  ▷ 'She won't want to talk to me,' (*I'm not worth enough*).
  ▷ 'Her mates will look down at me,' (*I'm not worth enough; things always go wrong*).
  ▷ 'I won't know what to say,' (*I'm not competent enough*).

When negative and limiting beliefs become active, our whole understanding of ourselves and the outside world changes. In such moments, confidence is lost. In Chapter 3 you learnt techniques to challenge distorted, irrational thoughts as they crop up. Continue to be aware when thinking negatively. By challenging distorted thoughts, you will change limiting beliefs over time.

Also, there is a faster way to change limiting beliefs. Let's go through it now.

Exercise 29

CHANGING LIMITING BELIEFS

▶ This exercise takes around 10 minutes.

▶ The aim is to see things differently in your mind.

▶ Read through the steps and familiarize yourself with them first.

▶ For some, using the rewind technique (see Chapter 7) on old memories first increases the efficacy of this exercise.

	Believing	Not believing
Visual imagery (yes / no):		
First or third person:		
Colour or black-and-white:		
Moving or still:		
Bright or dim:		
Fuzzy or focused:		
Shape:		
Life size, or smaller:		
Flat or 3-dimensional:		
Bordered or borderless:		
Close or distant:		

Location in your mind's eye: _____ _____

Sounds (yes / no): _____ _____

Loud or quiet: _____ _____

Pitch: _____ _____

Tone: _____ _____

Feelings (yes / no): _____ _____

Location in body: _____ _____

Movement and direction: _____ _____

Intensity: _____ _____

Colour (just guess): _____ _____

Physical sensations: _____ _____

Part 1 – How do you believe, or not?

When you truly *believe* something, what does it feel like?
The first part of this exercise involves understanding how
you experience feeling certainty – and then uncertainty.

1 Think of something positive you believe about yourself,
something you *know* to be true. It could be: being a
good listener, being a good friend, or being good at
your job or at a certain hobby. It needn't be anything
profound, just something you *know* you can do well.

2 In a moment, close your eyes and vividly imagine
doing that now (so – imagine being a good friend
or being good at your job, etc.) Spend a bit of time
relaxing into it. When you have it clear in your mind,
record your observations in the *believing* column
below.

3 If required, run the thought through your mind's eye several times, recording *how* you imagine it in the space above.

4 Next, think of something that you *just would not do*. Examples include: being horrible to somebody who you love, doing a particular job that just isn't you, being involved in a hobby that you cannot stand. Choose something you *fundamentally know* you would never do.

5 In a moment, close your eyes and imagine doing the thing you have chosen. Record your observations in the *not believing* column above. Again, run the thought through your mind several times, and be comprehensive with your answers.

That is the most difficult step out of the way. You now know how it looks and feels when experiencing believing – and not believing – something about yourself. This inventory is a key tool for changing negative beliefs.

Part 2 – Changing limiting beliefs

Our next step is to weaken the limiting beliefs that currently affect your confidence. This exercise will be particularly effective if you use it several times over the next week or two. For some, using this exercise after *desensitizing negative memories* works best. See Chapter 7 for more information.

1 Think of a situation where you've been struggling for confidence, despite using the techniques in this workbook. What is holding you back? Reflect on this a moment, is it:

▷ A fear of being judged, ridiculed, rejected, etc.? (I am not worth enough.)

▷ A fear of doing things wrong, not getting things perfect, finding yourself out of your comfort zone? (I am not competent enough.)

▷ A fear that, despite your best efforts, it's bound to go wrong? (Because things always go wrong.)

▷ Any combination of the three?

2 In a moment, close your eyes and vividly imagine *being* in that situation now. Spend a few moments to relax into it, and picture your lack of confidence in this context *fully*. Picture it vividly enough, and you should experience negative feelings in your stomach or chest.

3 The next step utilizes the *rewind technique*. For more information see Chapter 7, but the gist is to imagine yourself lacking confidence in the situation you have chosen, as if you were watching the scene on a CCTV camera: a small screen in your mind's eye, black-and-white, in the third person, and silent.

4 Play the scene in your mind's eye forwards, and then backwards – a couple of times at first (to build up how it looks and the order it plays in); then, play it forwards and backwards five times. Open your eyes when you have completed that. Then, close your eyes and play it for another five times. And so on...

5 Continue with this exercise for five minutes or so; soon it will feel as if you're watching *somebody else* on a TV screen in your mind.

Using the rewind technique on a specific situation where you lack confidence *softens things up* in readiness for change. Compared to using this technique on old memories, this step doesn't take long – just five minutes or so.

6 At this point, the visualization you have been working with will be easy to keep small, black-and-white, and third person in your mind's eye. The next step is very simple: imagine you can *snap!* the visualization in your mind so it takes on the attributes listed in the '*not believing*' column above. Take a minute or so to practise with that now.

→ In a moment, close your eyes, and see the visualization you have been working with.

→ Quickly *snap!* it so it takes on the qualities listed in the 'not believing' column above.

→ As you do this, aim to *feel* that it is unbelievable. Pay particular attention to your emotions.

→ Then open your eyes.

→ After a few attempts at this, speed it up and complete the process within a second or so.

7 Here, you are aiming to change the mental imagery so it looks and feels *unbelievable* – ten times in a row. Do it quickly, and open and close your eyes in between each time.

This step is designed to transform the old negative belief so you no longer believe it.

8 Now, how would you prefer to be in this situation? How would it look if you were confident? Imagine that you are competent, you have good self-worth, and you know it will turn out well. Close your eyes, and picture that now.

In a similar vein to step 5 above, take the visualization of this confident you, and *snap!* it in your mind so it takes on the attributes in the 'believing' column above. Close your eyes, and attempt this step now. When you get the hang of it, do it quickly, taking a second or two each time.

→ So, in a moment, close your eyes, and see the positive visualization you have been working with.

→ Quickly *snap!* it so it takes on the qualities listed in the 'believing' column above.

→ As you do this, aim to *feel* that it is believable. Pay particular attention to your emotions.

→ Then open your eyes.

→ After a few attempts at this, speed it up and complete the process within a second or so.

9 Good. Repeat the above step 10 times, opening and closing your eyes each time.

Well done! Despite looking complex, the process is very simple:

▶ 'Soften up' a negative belief by using the rewind technique on an imagined scenario where you lack confidence.
▶ Then, change the way this looks in your mind so you just *do not* believe it.
▶ Finally, imagine having confidence in the same situation, and change the way this looks in your mind so you *do* believe.

Use this exercise along with the techniques in Chapter 7, and your whole relationship with yourself will change.

Where to next?

Use the exercises in Chapters 7 and 8 together to form a process that will overcome even the most pernicious limiting belief:

▶ Identify a specific activating situation that still causes problems with your confidence.

▶ Do you have any old memories which are somehow *similar*? For example, if you are awkward in work, do you have memories of being awkward with classmates?

▶ If so, use the rewind technique on those memories until they are desensitized.

▶ Then, follow the belief change technique as outlined above.

▶ Finally, put yourself into the activating situation. You may still need to relax a little and spin positive feelings through your body, but it will be much easier to be confident *in the moment*.

Ideally, aim to set aside 20 minutes each day to carry out these exercises; 20 minutes is not a huge time commitment and, over the course of a couple of weeks, you will feel significant improvements in your confidence.

In the meantime, continue to use the techniques learnt so far in day-to-day life. In the next chapter we will turn our attention to *interpersonal confidence* – an essential ingredient to a happy and successful life.

Be more confident

→ What have I learnt from this chapter?

▶ _____

_____

_____

_____

▶ _____

_____

_____

_____

▶ _____

_____

_____

→ When can I practise these exercises?

▶ _____

_____

_____

▶ _____

_____

_____

▶ _____

_____

_____

Interpersonal confidence

In this chapter:

▶ *You will discover how to be confident around people.*

▶ *You will learn why we lack confidence with others, and how needlessly it holds us back in life.*

▶ *You will learn new techniques to build interpersonal confidence from the inside. Combine these exercises with practical experience, and your confidence around others will continue to grow.*

We tend to forget that people are as imperfect as ourselves. Instead, we lose confidence and feel anxious about their negative judgement. People who lack confidence tend to fear *rejection* more than anything else in life.

Have you ever looked down as you passed somebody on the street? Ask yourself: is there *really* any reason to do that? What is there to fear in the gaze of a fellow human being?

Opportunities in life come from people. If you can meet other people as their equal, able to exchange ideas and information, your life will be rich and fulfilled. If not, you will miss out. So, if you are struggling to communicate confidently, something needs to change.

→ How confident are you around people?

Take a quick look at the following questionnaire and answer as fully as possible.

Exercise 30

'I HAVE LACKED CONFIDENCE...'

▶ This simple exercise takes just a minute.

▶ The aim is to understand fully any problems you have with interpersonal confidence.

▶ Add suggestions of your own in the space provided (if required).

Work:

❑ When taking phone calls

❑ When attending a meeting

❑ When dealing with people 'in authority'

❑ When socializing with colleagues

❑ When networking

❑ In job interviews

Socially:

❑ With groups of people

❑ When friends of friends are present

❑ When approaching the opposite sex

❑ When speaking out in front of others

❑ When going into shops

❑ When walking down the street

❑ **When giving presentations**

❑ **With more attractive / successful people**

❑ **When asking questions in front of others**

❑ **When meeting people for the first time**

_____

_____

_____

_____

_____

_____

How many boxes did you tick?

▶ **Less than four boxes: your confidence with others seems good, but read on – you will still learn something.**

▶ **More than four boxes: you may have a problem with interpersonal confidence.**

▶ **More than eight boxes: your confidence with other people needs a _significant_ boost.**

WHY DO WE LACK CONFIDENCE WITH OTHERS?

Our judgement of our _self_ evolves as we go through life. Sometimes we feel comfortable in our own skin, and therefore we feel good amongst our peers. There is nothing to fear in their judgement.

Life doesn't always go well. Social anxiety kicks in when we lose sight of our gifts. Most people experience some social anxiety in their lifetime. If we put on weight, lose our job, or if our partner leaves us... who will brim with confidence then?

People are just people. They rarely present any *real* danger to us, yet we hide our true selves, just in case. Overcoming this fear depends on a healthy relationship with oneself and feeling *capable* around others. When these two conditions are met we see people as equals. Confidence follows, as we shall see.

CASE STUDY – REBECCA

Rebecca, a ticket office worker from Portsmouth, was overweight and unhappy. Each day she dressed for work, her mind full of automatic negative thoughts:

- ▶ 'You fat mess!'
- ▶ 'You're so fat and ugly...'
- ▶ 'Urgh, look at the state of you. It makes me sick to look at it you fat cow!'

(We discussed in Chapter 3 how automatic negative thinking damages confidence. These examples illustrate the point clearly.)

Over time, Rebecca's automatic negative thinking became worse. She didn't just think these thoughts, she muttered them under her breath. Once bubbly and outgoing, Rebecca was now quiet and withdrawn. Her confidence around others could not be any worse, and she had come to despise the mirror.

An old friend, visiting from out of town, was staying at her house for the weekend. Rebecca reluctantly agreed to go out for a meal, and was deciding what to wear. Out of habit, she started saying the usual insults to herself. Her friend was shocked; *why was she talking to herself like that?*

Rebecca broke down and cried. Her friend listened patiently and comforted her, finally interrupting to make an important point.

'Would you say those things to me?' Her friend, never slim, was a couple of dress sizes larger than Rebecca. 'Of course not!' Rebecca was appalled at the idea of treating her old friend in that way...

A GOOD RELATIONSHIP WITH YOURSELF

Can you see the distortion in Rebecca's thinking? She talked to herself in a way she would never talk to others. To have a good relationship with yourself means being kinder, free of harsh judgement, and realizing that – whatever your flaws, weaknesses and limitations – you are still a human being, the same as everybody else.

Judge yourself unfairly, and you will feel threatened by the judgement of others:

▶ If I think badly of myself, then other people must think the same.

▶ If other people see who I am, they will reject me, and that hurts.

▶ If people reject me, it will confirm the bad things I think about myself, and that would hurt even more.

We do not have to be conscious of this *inner logic* – it affects us on an unconscious, emotional level. If you irrationally feel anxious around others, there is a strong possibility that you fear judgement and rejection. In such cases, rejection is an abstract, generalized idea based on a skewed self-perception. Our view of ourselves is complex and rarely fair.

Have you ever felt inferior when talking to a group of people? Is there really any cause to worry about what people think? We dazzle ourselves with the beauty, intelligence and success of others, and forget that every human being has their own weaknesses and flaws – no matter what importance *you* place on their strengths.

Are you making progress with the exercises in the previous two chapters? Desensitizing old memories, and changing limiting beliefs (especially: I'm not worth enough) is key to improving your relationship with yourself. Weaken those limiting beliefs, and your anxiety will decrease. Pay special attention to difficult social experiences in your past, and your beliefs in social contexts.

In addition, use this simple exercise, once or twice a day for the next month.

Exercise 31

BUILDING KINDNESS TOWARDS YOURSELF

► This exercise takes 1 minute.

► The aim is to look at yourself with 'fresh eyes'.

► It takes a little time to get used to it – persevere and it will really pay off.

► Familiarize yourself with the steps before practising.

1 Stand in front of a mirror. If you are body conscious, do not hide from the reality of who you are.

2 Close your eyes, and imagine a trusted friend or relative in your mind's eye. Picture them vividly speaking to you. Hear their voice (not your voice) telling you: *they are your friend, they love you, and they want you to be happy and well in life.*

3 Spend about a minute doing this, and know that it is true; they are a trusted person in your life and they care – accept this reality. Imagine they are there with you, and let yourself feel *loved*.

4 Then, open your eyes, and look at yourself in the mirror. Stay relaxed, and remember that this is what everyone else sees, including – especially even – those people who really care. You cannot be all bad if people love you.

This exercise only takes a minute; use it when getting dressed, in the afternoon at some point, and before you go to bed. Sometimes we just need to learn to be kind to ourselves as we set out to achieve our goals. Do not skip past it – that is just another form of unkindness.

SELF-EFFICACY AND INTERPERSONAL CONFIDENCE

Self-efficacy, in a social context, refers to our ability to get on with others. Know that you can competently hold a conversation, and you will feel more confident around people. If you fear that you're incapable of making a good impression, then your confidence is bound to falter. Do any of these thoughts seem familiar?

▶ They can see how nervous I am.

▶ They don't like me.

▶ I can't say that.

▶ I'm boring / stupid / shouldn't be here.

▶ I'm don't fit in.

▶ Think of something to say!

▶ Everything I say sounds stupid.

Confidence comes – in part – from competence. Practise communicating with others and your competence will increase. Unfortunately, people who lack confidence tend to shy away and keep themselves safe, rejecting the behaviour that improves things in the long run.

→ Communicating confidently

To be confident around others, you need to do three simple things:

▶ Physically and mentally relax, easing anxiety away and challenging negative thinking.

▶ Spend time interacting with people, because some confidence comes from *competence*.

▶ Become less self-conscious and more focused on what people are saying.

Let's go through some exercises that will help.

PRACTISING BEING CONFIDENT WITH OTHERS

The only way to improve your interpersonal confidence is to be in social situations. For some, this might seem terrifying. Don't panic! We're going to start small and work our way up.

There are plenty of opportunities to engage with people in day-to-day life. Improving your social skills means making the most of these opportunities:

▶ You will get better at learning how to relax around others.

▶ You will get better at knowing what to say.

▶ You will get better at focusing on other people, rather than on yourself.

Improve in these three areas and your interpersonal confidence will grow.

IDENTIFYING OPPORTUNITIES TO COMMUNICATE CONFIDENTLY

In your day-to-day life, you have ample opportunity to communicate with people. Chatting with colleagues, approaching bosses, visiting friends, asking strangers for the time, making small-talk with shopkeepers and taxi drivers... For most of us, life is a succession of interpersonal exchanges.

List five *new* opportunities you can make to converse with people. Aim to get out of your comfort zone, even just a little. They do not have to be terrifying situations, just challenging enough to your current level of confidence. List your five opportunities in the space provided.

Over the next few weeks, I can practise confident communication in the following situations:

1. _____

   _____

2. _____

   _____

3. _____

   _____

4. _____

   _____

5. _____

   _____

Did you think of five new situations? You might feel anxious when you look at this list – and that's the first thing we need to change. Relax, and you'll be fine. Remember, *there is no lion...*

The first thing you need to overcome is performance anxiety – fear in anticipation of social interaction. The following, simple exercise works well for this. It builds on previous techniques, and is very straightforward.

Exercise 32

PREPARING TO SOCIALIZE

▶ This exercise takes 5 minutes.

▶ The aim is to relax and get yourself into a confident state.

▶ Use this exercise before or during social situations.

▶ Familiarize yourself with the steps beforehand.

1 Breathe in slowly through your nose, mentally counting to five as you do so.

2 Then, slowly exhale through your mouth, mentally telling yourself, *'they're just people – not lions... I can deal with this!'*

3 Repeat these steps three times. As you do so, make sure that you relax your neck and shoulders, your jaw, your back, your torso and your feet. Stress is often carried in these areas of the body.

4 Is the voice in your head nervous or confident? Use your confident inner voice (see Chapter 3) when speaking to yourself in your own mind. If you get automatic, negative thoughts popping into your mind (*'I won't know what to say', 'They won't like me', 'I'll make a fool of myself,'* etc.) then challenge those thoughts with something confident:

  ▷ I'll be fine – they're just people.
  ▷ They aren't perfect either!
  ▷ Just relax, it's only practice. I don't have to be perfect.
  ▷ Nobody is judging me, and if they were it really doesn't matter.
  ▷ I'm as good as anyone else here.
  ▷ Listen – there is no lion! Relax!

And so forth – with practice, you'll be able to come up with your own coping thoughts. For now, text yourself a few of these coping thoughts so you have them to hand when needed.

5 Each time you exhale, practise the spinning feelings exercise we used in Chapter 5. Within moments, anxiety and resistance can be effectively eased away.

6 Are any negative visual images flashing through your mind? If so, squash them down (as we practised in Chapter 3) and replace them with positive images; see yourself at ease, effortlessly communicating with others.

7 Keep this up – breathing and relaxing, spinning negative feelings, changing spoken and visual thoughts – for around a minute or so. Relax into it: with practice it will be easy.

Practise this exercise repeatedly over the next few days. Spend a little time each day thinking about social situations; as you do, go through this exercise several times and get to grips with it. You know all of the techniques by now, it is just a matter of using them together.

Use this exercise before engaging in any social situation. Anxiety generally eases off after a couple of minutes have passed. This exercise will help until then.

THE GOAL OF SOCIAL SITUATIONS

Earlier in this chapter, you identified opportunities to practise being around others, and you now have an exercise to overcome anxiety in social situations. To improve your interpersonal confidence, put yourself into these situations and get some solid experience.

When in social situations, aim to do the following:

1 To begin, use the exercise above (*preparing to socialize*) to overcome performance anxiety.

2 Then, depending on the situation you're in:
   ▷ Approach the person you're going to speak to.
   ▷ When you speak or introduce yourself, people are bound to look – be prepared and breathe through it. People looking at you doesn't mean anything bad is going to happen.
   ▷ If required, offer a confident sounding '*Hello*' or '*Hi*', and a **smile**.
   ▷ If required, take your opportunity to contribute when it arises.
   ▷ It can help to rehearse what you're going to say beforehand.
   ▷ If anxiety rises, use the 'preparing to socialize' technique once more.

▷ Remember your confident inner voice? It can also be your confident outer voice. Try speaking out loud with it and become familiar with how it sounds.

3 Complete this process in *five* social situations, and you'll get the hang of it.

4 With all social situations, the goal is to be *in the moment* with others. Over time, you will be able to focus more and more on what people are saying, and less and less on how you're feeling.

It's simple, really – but it does require experience. Transcend anxiety and negative thinking and you'll find it easy to relax socially, especially when the *kindness exercise* in this chapter fully kicks in. So – best foot forward, and engage with your practice opportunities daily.

The most important thing to remember is: there is no rejection, at least not in the way you think. Aim to be yourself; sometimes you will fit in, at other times less so. It is not important providing you are true to yourself. Ease past your fear of judgement, and everything will change.

Exercise 33

THE ABCS OF YOUR INTERPERSONAL CONFIDENCE

▶ This exercise takes 10 minutes or so to write up.

▶ The aim is to learn from your experiences by reflecting on them.

1 Choose one of the social situations identified earlier in this chapter, and use the *preparing to socialize* exercise until you feel more relaxed about it.

2 Then, put yourself into the social situation, using the skills learnt so far to keep anxiety at bay. The key is to relax. Keep breathing, and keep using the coping thoughts (see above) – people *are* just people.

3 Once you have practised being confident in that situation, make a note of your thoughts and feelings, and the techniques you used. Record as much as you can.

4 Then, transfer your notes to the five ABC tables below. Aim to complete at least *five* social experiences before moving on to the next chapter.

Remember to use the skills you have learnt so far; it will get easier with practice.

MY ABC TABLES – INTERPERSONAL EXERCISES

Activating situation:	
Belief:	
Consequences:	
Helpful techniques used:	

Activating situation:	
Belief:	
Consequences:	
Helpful techniques used:	

Activating situation:	
Belief:	
Consequences:	
Helpful techniques used:	

Activating situation:	
Belief:	
Consequences:	
Helpful techniques used:	

Activating situation:	
Belief:	
Consequences:	
Helpful techniques used:	

When it comes to people, it *really* is all about practice. Use the techniques you have learnt so far, and you will find your feet.

Where to next?

Interacting with people seems difficult when we lack confidence. However, put yourself into social situations and use the skills you have learnt so far – it will be easier than you imagine. Remember to progress the work from the previous two chapters. *If social confidence is a problem, prioritize difficult social memories and beliefs*.

Even as you progress, you may still find yourself struggling with eye contact, body language and feeling *on the spot*. In the next chapter you will discover techniques to counter safety behaviour – in and out of social settings.

For now, practise what you have learnt. Record your experiences in the ABC tables above as you progress. Learning to relax before – and during – social situations is the key. Master that, and everything else will be easy.

Be more confident

→ What have I learnt from this chapter?

▶ _____

_____

_____

▶ _____

_____

_____

▶ _____

_____

_____

→ When can I practise these exercises?

▶ _____

_____

_____

▶ _____

_____

_____

▶ _____

_____

_____

10 Overcoming safety behaviours

In this chapter:
- ► *You will learn how safety behaviours maintain low confidence.*
- ► *Safety behaviours are born of fear. You will understand how to identify and change such behaviours, including in social contexts.*
- ► *You will explore techniques designed to mentally rehearse how you'd like to be. Overcome the unnecessary urge to keep yourself 'safe', and your journey towards better confidence is almost complete.*

Confidence is a multifaceted concept. Even as a person's confidence improves, certain situations still trigger a desire to *run away*. This desire can be obvious or it can be subtle, and there is a good chance that, despite the improvements you have made so far, you still avoid certain things.

When we repeatedly do something, it becomes automated. This is generally a good thing. It would be a chore if you had to learn how to tie your shoelaces each morning. Instead, based on repetition, you can tie your shoelaces with your eyes closed (try it!)

However, not all habits are helpful. Even if you have overcome negative thinking, learnt to feel more confident and started to believe in yourself, certain habitual behaviours may hold you back. Let's explore how.

→ Safety behaviours

Imagine a shy young man at a party. He avoids eye contact, struggles to talk to people and leaves early. Disappointed (and perhaps relieved), he comes to the conclusion, '*At least I went. Maybe it'll be better next time...*' And yet, despite this, a negative belief has been reinforced, '*I knew I wouldn't be confident enough to socialize*'. This is not a conscious thought; it is more of a feeling. Consider this for a moment. It is possible for us to hold two conclusions at the same time.

Which of these two conclusions will carry the most weight: the barely believed optimistic thought at the front of his mind, or the emotional conclusion at the back of his mind? You would have to think the latter; the safety behaviours (avoiding eye contact, leaving early, etc.) have confirmed his lack of confidence, maintaining it or even making it worse.

So, safety behaviours can be quite subtle:

▶ A person wants to approach their boss for a pay rise; every time they avoid broaching it, the idea becomes more terrifying.

▶ As a result of a crash, a motorist avoids motorways, taking 'A' roads instead. Each time motorways are avoided, the motorist's lack of confidence is reinforced.

▶ A person attends an exercise class for the first time, but throughout they don't really try; they leave with the idea that, '*it's just not for me*'. Confidence is lost...

The first two examples suggest the need to escape or avoid. At other times (e.g. in the third example) we just give up, *reducing activity* and letting ourselves fall behind. Some behaviours may *seem* to keep us safe, but they just reinforce the idea, '*I can't do it*'. Instead we become stuck and miss out.

Let's look at these behaviours in more detail. There is space for your own notes – leave that blank for now.

ESCAPE AND AVOIDANCE

Avoiding or escaping situations really damages confidence.
As we have learnt, avoidance and escape can be subtle,
leaving us prone to similar reactions in future.

Typical safety escape / avoidance behaviour includes:

▶ Turning down the opportunity to do something you
would like to do.
▶ Racing through tasks so that you can 'escape' it as soon
as possible.
▶ Wearing certain clothes to avoid being judged for
whatever reason.

→My examples of this safety behaviour:_____

_____

_____

_____

_____

→What I can do instead:_____

_____

_____

_____

_____

→Where I can practise the new behaviour:_____

_____

_____

_____

REDUCTION OF ACTIVITY

At its worst, reduced activity can mean depression. *It is important to seek professional advice from your GP if you suspect you are depressed.* Socially withdrawing, or avoiding projects and tasks, limits your opportunity for reward and social acceptance – vital factors in maintaining confidence. This loss then confirms our negative beliefs, further reducing our ability to feel confident in the future.

Typical confidence-based reduced activity includes:

▶ Losing interest in the things you'd like to do, if you felt confident enough.

▶ Giving up on improving your circumstances.

▶ Strong thoughts about being stuck and hopeless.

➡ My examples of this safety behaviour:_____

_____

_____

_____

_____

➡ What I can do instead:_____

_____

_____

_____

_____

➜ Where I can practise the new behaviour:_____

_____

_____

_____

PERFECTIONISM

At first glance, it might seem paradoxical that low confidence results in perfectionism. However, lacking confidence causes many of us to yearn for perfection – as if to demonstrate our worth. As things can never be perfect, avoidance behaviours and self-fulfilling prophecies follow. Perfectionism is one of the subtlest and most damaging safety behaviours.

Typical perfectionist behaviour includes:

▶ Alternating between fantastic ideas of achieving the impossible, followed by a sense of being able to achieve nothing.
▶ Constantly viewing achievements as not being good enough.
▶ Procrastinating over the smallest action or decision.

➜ My examples of this safety behaviour:_____

_____

_____

_____

➜ What I can do instead:_____

_____

_____

_____

→Where I can practise the new behaviour:_____

_____

_____

_____

How many of these behaviours do you recognize? Let's look at how they can be overcome.

Exercise 34

IDENTIFYING SAFETY BEHAVIOURS

▶ This exercise takes about a minute.

▶ The aim is to identify safety behaviours that still hold you back.

1 Go through each safety behaviour (above) again, and write down your own examples; think about recent times when you have avoided things, felt anxious, etc. Write your examples down in the corresponding category above. You may write the same behaviour in multiple categories – they are not mutually exclusive.

2 What confident behaviour could you do instead? Remember: safety behaviours maintain low confidence even if our thoughts, feelings and beliefs are improving. Write down how you'd prefer to be in those circumstances.

3 Finally, think about situations in day-to-day life where your safety behaviours might typically occur and write them down: these situations are your opportunity to practise being more confident.

Here is an example to get you started:

Perfectionism

▶ **My examples of this safety behaviour:**
I wanted to ask my boyfriend to move in with me, but the night

was rubbish (he was really tired and more interested in watching

the TV) so I didn't ask him in the end.

▶ **What I can do instead:**
Dismiss the negative thoughts (he doesn't want to talk about

this now), stay positive and overcome the anxiety.

▶ **Where I can practise the new behaviour:**
We are going for dinner next Thursday – I'll try and be really

confident then – it'll prove I can do it!

In this example, we can see that a setback caused old doubts to reappear, leading to avoidance behaviour (avoiding asking the question).

Learning to recognize safety behaviour as it crops up means overcoming obstacles and growing in confidence. Keep in mind how damaging such behaviour is, and aim to do the *very opposite*:

▶ If you want to avoid doing something (or escape from something) – then do it.
▶ If you want to reduce your level of activity and hold yourself back – go for it and get involved.
▶ If you want to make something perfect – aim to do it anyway, even though it's not perfect.

And so on...

So: the key to overcoming safety behaviour is to do the very opposite of what you'd *like* to do! Let's look at a technique that is designed especially to help.

→ Overcoming safety behaviours

It is best to focus on just one or two behaviours and eliminate them a step at a time. Trying to do too much will cause your progress to stall.

Exercise 35

OVERCOMING SAFETY BEHAVIOUR

▶ This exercise comes in two parts.

▶ Part 1 takes around 5–10 minutes; part 2 takes just a minute or two.

▶ Use the exercise frequently, ideally once per day.

▶ Focus on just one behaviour at a time.

▶ Read through the steps first and familiarize yourself with them.

Part 1 – overcoming anxiety

Safety behaviours reflect *anxious desire*; the first part of the exercise weakens anxiety.

1 Choose a safety behaviour you want to be rid of. Close your eyes and imagine carrying out that behaviour *in your mind's eye*. Picture it as clearly as you can, preferably in one of the scenarios identified in the previous exercise. In your imagination, watch how you behave, and consider how you think and feel as well. Ease yourself into it, and spend a bit of time making the detail clear.

2 Change the way this looks in your mind's eye, so you:

▶ **Picture the scene on a TV screen in your mind.**

▶ **Picture it in the third person view, so you're watching yourself from a distance.**

▶ **Make the picture black-and-white, speeded up slightly, and quite small.**

▶ **Play this visualization forwards (from start to finish), so you get the gist of what is going on, and then backwards (from the end, back to the beginning).**

You will recognize this technique from previous chapters. For a fuller description, see the 'rewind technique' in Chapter 7.

3 If you feel anxious, use the spinning feelings technique to ease it away (see Chapter 5).

4 In your mind's eye, keep the visualization small, black-and-white, distant and third person. To begin, the image will try to become large, colourful and in the first person. Just keep playing it forwards and backwards until it settles down – it will only take a minute or two.

5 After a while, the visualization will speed up. Keep playing it forwards and backwards, until it starts to go really fast. If you feel anxious or resistant, breathe

slowly and use the spinning feelings technique to ease the sensations away.

6 Eventually, you'll feel very detached from the visualization; it will feel as if you're watching somebody else on a TV screen in your mind. At that point, tell yourself – using your confident voice – '*I am free of that now*'. Then, open your eyes; part 1 is complete.

This should take around 5–10 minutes.

Part 2 – rehearsing confident behaviour

How would it be if, in this scenario, you were very confident? Part 2 of this exercise involves mentally rehearsing positive behaviour. Use this exercise to prepare yourself in advance. Also, you can use this part of the exercise to inject positivity into *any given moment*.

1 If you were to do the opposite of the safety behaviour you are working with, what would you do?

→ If you would normally avoid something, what would the opposite be?

→ If you would normally escape from something, how would the opposite look?

→ If you would normally reduce your activity or strive for perfectionism, how would it be if you did the opposite?

2 Think of somebody you know who would *absolutely not* use safety behaviours; somebody who would be confident in the situation you are thinking about.

3 Close your eyes and imagine that person in the same situation.

→ Imagine how they'd feel and act.

→ Imagine what is going through their mind.

→ What would their body language be like? How would they address others?

→ How confident are they?

4 Imagine this vividly for 30 seconds or so, getting the full picture.

5 Then, change the picture so it is *you* thinking, feeling, and acting in this positive and confident way. Don't change anything else: watch yourself be exactly as they would be. Watch yourself do exactly what they would do.

6 Tell yourself, using your confident voice, '*this is how I will be!*' As you do so, imagine being there, looking through your own eyes, in the moment, thinking, feeling and behaving with great confidence.

Athletes use this technique to improve their confidence. Stepping into somebody else's shoes (and making those shoes your own) means you're *rehearsing* how you want things to be. This technique is particularly powerful.

Overcoming anxiety – and mentally rehearsing how you'd rather be – will weaken the urge to carry out safety behaviours. As this behaviour is habitual, you may still get a *small urge* to escape or avoid (or whichever) in the moment.

This urge will be easy to override, and it will pass. Decide to do the opposite, the *positive* action, and your confidence will continue to improve.

→ Social safety behaviours

People who lack confidence often keep themselves safe in social situations, usually by deploying subtle, often unconscious, techniques.

Some social safety behaviour is obvious, for example: crossing the street to avoid somebody or sitting silently in a group of people. Social safety behaviour can also be subtle; any behaviour designed to keep people *at arm's length* can be a problem.

Read through the following examples – tick any behaviour you recognize from your own social interactions.

▶ Avoiding (or feeling deeply uncomfortable during) eye contact. ❑

▶ Crossing the street or staying away from certain areas to avoid people you know. ❑

▶ Being overly polite or always agreeing with people. ❑

▶ Cleverly deflecting topics of conversation away from personal matters. ❑

▶ Making excuses for anxious behaviour. ❑

▶ Saying 'yes' to everything, even when you don't want to. ❑

▶ Wearing certain clothes to avoid being judged for whatever reason. ❑

▶ Over-rehearsing what you'll say to people when asked. ❑

▶ Under-rehearsing what you'll say to people when asked. ❑

▶ Staying on the edge of groups, saying nothing. ❑

▶ Giving vague, short answers when asked questions. ❑

▶ Managing conversations so they remain safe. ❑

▶ Fidgeting or shrinking within yourself, altering your physical presence. ❑

This behaviour is designed to deflect scrutiny – we learn to fear prying eyes and minds. It isn't a rational or logical process, and it doesn't matter who is doing the scrutinizing; it is not about their judgement – this behaviour is born of our own fear.

Although social safety behaviour tends to be subtle, it is still very damaging. So, list five safety behaviours you would like to remove using the techniques in this chapter.

Over time, I will eradicate the following safety behaviour:

1._____

_____

2._____

_____

3._____

_____

4._____

_____

5._____

_____

These behaviours *are* a problem for your confidence, and it is well worth changing them. The exercise 'overcoming safety behaviour' will help. When carrying out Part 2 of that exercise, imagine a really confident person (in social situations) and draw on them for inspiration.

Exercise 36

THE ABCS OF SAFETY BEHAVIOURS

▶ This exercise takes 10 minutes or so to write up.

▶ The aim is to learn from your experiences by reflecting on them.

1 Before any situation where safety behaviour might happen, follow this process:

▷ A day or two beforehand, use the 'overcoming safety behaviour' exercise in this chapter. Focus on changing just one behaviour at a time. If social safety behaviours are a problem, prioritize those.

▷ The moment just before entering a situation is critical; be especially mindful of your thoughts and anxiety levels at this time. Use the techniques in Chapters 3 and 4 as required.

▷ The second part of the exercise above, 'rehearsing confident behaviour' is particularly helpful just before and during any difficult situation.

▷ Instead of focusing on the urge to escape, avoid, etc., relax and use coping thoughts to help.

▷ Nothing serious is going to happen.

▷ It's just anxiety – ease through it.

▷ I'll survive, no matter how they react.

▷ I can cope with whatever happens.

Within minutes, the urge to keep yourself safe will have eased, and you'll be fine.

2 After practising overriding safety behaviours, make a note of your thoughts and feelings, the techniques you used, and the outcomes achieved. Record as much as you can.

3 Then, transfer your notes to the five ABC tables below. Aim to complete all five before moving on to the next chapter.

In Exercise 35 (Overcoming safety behaviour) you identified several opportunities to practise being more confident. Focus on those scenarios and use the techniques in this chapter to change the way you do things.

MY ABC TABLES – SAFETY BEHAVIOUR EXERCISES

Activating situation:	
Belief:	
Consequences:	
Helpful techniques used:	

Activating situation:	
Belief:	
Consequences:	
Helpful techniques used:	

Activating situation:	
Belief:	
Consequences:	
Helpful techniques used:	

Activating situation:	
Belief:	
Consequences:	
Helpful techniques used:	

Activating situation:	
Belief:	
Consequences:	
Helpful techniques used:	

Remember – safety behaviour contributes to low confidence and robs you of your chance to outgrow it. Practise, experiment and give yourself the time you need to learn.

Where to next?

Changing safety behaviour is a key step to increasing confidence. For the next week or so, practise using the techniques in this chapter and eradicate one safety behaviour at a time. Do not attempt to tackle it all at once. You will have much more success if you focus on just one change to begin with.

Compared with some of the exercises in this workbook, you should find this relatively straightforward; the key is to use the 'overcoming safety behaviour' in advance (where possible), and ease past any urges you have to avoid, escape, give up or strive for impossible perfection. Relax, take your time and learn as you go.

In the next chapter, we will turn our attention to goal-setting. You almost have everything you need to change your life for good.

Be more confident

→ What have I learnt from this chapter?

▶ _____

_____

_____

▶ _____

_____

_____

▶ _____

_____

_____

→ When can I practise these exercises?

▶ _____

_____

_____

▶ _____

_____

_____

▶ _____

_____

_____

11 Setting your confidence goal

In this chapter:
▶ *You will learn how to set a SMART confidence goal – your overall target for greater confidence.*
▶ *SMART goals are measurable and achievable. By setting in-depth goals you give yourself the best chance of success.*
▶ *You bought this workbook for a reason – to be more confident in life. Focus on your goal, and you will achieve just that.*

So far, you have learnt various techniques to build your confidence, from changing your thoughts to changing your feelings, and from improving your beliefs to freeing yourself from confidence-sapping safety behaviour. Each chapter of this workbook has focused on a different aspect of confidence. Now, let's tie this all together and work towards a *confidence goal*.

Even if you have read about goal-setting elsewhere – read on. The exercises in this chapter are essential to completing your confidence programme.

→ What is a goal?

Put simply, a goal is a *desired result*; an end-point arrived at via your own thought, action and persistence. It is widely accepted that setting goals is key to achieving success:

- ▶ Your goal reflects your desire – it will focus and motivate you.
- ▶ Knowing your desired outcome will stop you from drifting.
- ▶ Progression towards your goal will feel good, building confidence in itself.

Let's go through the process now.

SETTING THE RIGHT GOAL

Previously you completed a checklist, highlighting those areas where your confidence could be improved. Turn to Chapter 2 now and review your answers. Which of these areas are still applicable?

You may wish to tackle everything in one go, but overwhelming yourself is a sure-fire way to fail. Take things a step at a time – it is the only way to learn. Before you decide on your goal, let's look at goal-setting in more detail.

What constitutes a good *confidence goal*? To start with, a good goal should be SMART:

- ▶ **Specific steps:** what steps will take you towards your goal? You should know *what* is expected, *who* is involved, and *where* the goal will be achieved.
  - ▷ 'I am going to be more confident in meetings,' is not specific.
  - ▷ 'I am going to speak confidently three times in the weekly team meeting,' is specific.
- ▶ **Measurable outcomes:** how will you know when your goal has been accomplished? What will be different about your thoughts, your feelings and your behaviour?
  - ▷ 'I am going to be more confident with my friends,' is not easily measurable.

▷ 'I am going to feel comfortable when accepting compliments from friends,' is measurable.

▶ **Attainable:** for a goal to be attainable, it needs to stretch you while remaining realistic. How do you know your goal is realistic?

▷ 'I am going to become more confident than anyone I know,' might be difficult to achieve.

▷ 'I am going to interact confidently with all my friends,' is achievable with practice.

▶ **Relevant:** achieving your confidence goal should feel exciting. Aim for something important to you. Build the confidence to do something amazing!

▷ 'I want to be confident enough to go self-employed,' may be relevant to your aspirations.

▷ 'I want to be confident enough to work as a road sweeper,' probably isn't...

▶ **Time-based:** when will the goal be achieved by? This week? This month? This year? Setting the right deadline for your goal is key.

▷ 'I want to be confident with my boss at some point soon,' does not include a deadline.

▷ 'I want to be confident with my boss by my birthday,' sets a firm deadline to work towards.

Defining a SMART goal gives you the best chance of achieving it.

ABOUT SPECIFIC STEPS

Knowing the action you need to take increases your chances of success. Take a look at the following examples:

▶ I am going to build the confidence to *be more assertive*. I will take the following steps:

▷ I will be more assertive with my hairdresser.

▷ I will join my local writing group.

> ▷ I will tell Sue at work to stop making her hurtful comments!

> ▷ I will disagree with my partner without becoming emotional.

▶ I am going to build the confidence to change my job. I will take the following steps:

> ▷ I will update my CV.

> ▷ I will send off at least four job applications per week.

> ▷ I will speak to my friend, Claire, about opportunities in her office.

> ▷ I will enrol on the marketing course I read about.

> ▷ I will speak to my colleagues more each day.

Specific steps can relate directly or indirectly to your goal. For example:

▶ Building the confidence to send off job applications *directly* relates to changing career.

▶ Speaking to more colleagues in the office *indirectly* contributes towards changing career; it still counts because it is a useful, confidence-building activity.

What specific steps, direct and indirect, will take you towards your confidence goal? Knowing these steps is the only way you can succeed.

ABOUT MEASURABLE OUTCOMES

To measure progress towards your goal, you need to know what you expect to happen, and the outcomes you hope to achieve. Often these outcomes tie into the specific steps you will take:

▶ I will know when I have the confidence to *be more assertive* because:

> ▷ I will have the confidence to tell people what I want (such as being more honest with my hairdresser or telling Sue that I don't like her sniping).

> ▷ I will feel confident enough to try new things.

> ▷ I will be able to express my opinions in my relationship without becoming defensive.

▶ I will know when I have the confidence to *change my job* because:

> ▷ I will be going for interviews.

> ▷ I will be more confident around people at work.

> ▷ I will feel optimistic about future career opportunities.

Determine measurable outcomes, and you increase your connection to your goal. *'I'll feel more confident,'* is too vague. Instead, think about your thoughts, your feelings and your behaviour; think about how, when and where you'll be more confident. Think about how it will look to others. There is a difference between these two examples:

▶ I will feel more confident around new people.

And:

▶ I will feel more relaxed (and less anxious) when meeting new people.

▶ My body language will be more open around my friends.

▶ I'll no longer censor my thoughts for being too stupid or boring.

▶ I'll focus on what people are saying.

Knowing what you want to happen means knowing what to aim for – it is important to keep this in mind.

ABOUT SETTING DEADLINES

A goal without a deadline is just a dream. To increase your chances of success, you want focus and motivation. Having a deadline helps – without it, you run the risk of procrastination. A good deadline is not too close, nor too distant. Instead, it should be appropriate to the confidence goal you have chosen. You could consider either of the following:

- ▶ **Make significant progress for the next month,** e.g. focus on your confidence goal each day for the next month.
- ▶ **Achieve your goal by a certain date,** e.g. aim to have attained your confidence goal by the end of the year, your birthday or whenever...

Selecting the right deadline depends on the nature of the goal. If your goal is to build the confidence to start a new hobby, then selecting a significant date (e.g. your birthday) makes a lot of sense. You have a memorable date to work towards.

Some goals require daily focus: becoming more confident with colleagues, for example. Setting a time-frame based around monthly blocks would work well – calendar months also provide useful deadlines.

When you define important steps, it pays to set deadlines for those as well. The main thing to remember when setting a deadline is to **be bold!** Go for it, and set yourself a challenge.

CASE STUDY – MARK

Mark, a 33-year-old office worker, wants the confidence to start a new relationship. He has been single for over a year, and most of his friends have now settled down. He feels a bit left behind. Opportunities to meet single women seem limited, and the idea of internet dating leaves him terrified.

To begin, Mark filled out a *goal worksheet*.

GOAL WORKSHEET

As of today, I am building the confidence to:

Start a new relationship with somebody I really like.

Specific steps: What action are you going to take?

▶ What exactly will you have the confidence to do?

▶ Where will the goal be achieved? (In work? At home? In several locations?)

▶ Who else, if anyone, does the goal involve?

I am going to sign up to an internet dating site.

I'm going to join a local socializing group to make new friends.

I'll ask my friend Alison to help me with some new clothes and grooming tips.

Measurable outcomes: How will you know when you have reached the goal?

▶ What will you see or hear when you have achieved your goal?

▶ What quantity or numbers can you put on the outcome?

► What specific bad feelings will go away? What good feelings will you feel?

I'll feel better about the way I look.

I'll have an internet dating profile that helps me meet people.

I will be going on one or two dates per week, hopefully with people I want to spend time with!

Relevant: How is this goal significant to you?

► Why is it important to you?

► What would it mean if you didn't achieve the goal?

► What would it mean if you did achieve the goal?

Meeting somebody new is really important to me. Work is going well and I like my

life – I'd just like somebody to share it with. If I don't do this now I'll feel more and more

frustrated with myself – it feels like I am being left behind!

Time-based: When will you reach this goal?

► What time limit can you put on this goal?

► Habits take 3–4 weeks to form. How long do you need to work at your goal for?

I hope to have met the right person by my birthday (5 months away).

I would like to join a local social group and create an internet dating profile (gulp!)

within the next 4 weeks.

Reading through Mark's notes, we can see he has completed the following:

▶ Stated his goal.

▶ Described the required steps to achieve his confidence goal, where he'll achieve it and who will help.

▶ Described the measure of success.

▶ Explained why the goal is important, and what will come of it.

▶ Set an achievable deadline for the goal, as well as a deadline for an important step (creating an internet dating profile).

Goal-setting is an art. At this stage aim to get a reasonable amount of detail down on paper. In the example above, Mark hasn't gone into forensic detail, but he has been quite specific. When it comes to *your* goal, aim to be specific as well.

Exercise 37

SETTING YOUR 'CONFIDENCE GOAL'

▶ This exercise will take 10–15 minutes.

▶ The aim is to identify a confidence goal that you would love to achieve.

Review the checklist in Chapter 2 and decide on the area where you'd most like more confidence.

▶ Set a goal that will stretch you, but which is achievable.

▶ Make sure the goal is important to you.

▶ Ideally, choose a confidence goal that you can achieve in the next month or two.

Fill out the worksheet below. **Do not skip this step!** It cannot be stressed enough how important it is to get your goals down on paper.

GOAL WORKSHEET

As of today, I am building the confidence to:

_____

_____

_____

Specific steps: What exactly are you going to achieve?

▶ What exactly will you have the confidence to do?

▶ Where will the goal be achieved? (In work? At home? In several locations?)

▶ Who else, if anyone, does the goal involve?

_____

_____

_____

_____

_____

_____

_____

_____

Measurable outcomes: How will you know when you have reached the goal?

► What will you see or hear when you have achieved your goal?

► What quantity or numbers can you put on the outcome?

► What specific bad feelings will go away? What good feelings will you feel?

_____

_____

_____

_____

_____

_____

_____

_____

Relevant: How is this goal significant to you?

► Why is it important to you?

► What would it mean if you didn't achieve the goal?

► What would it mean if you did achieve the goal?

_____

_____

_____

_____

_____

_____

_____

_____

Time-based: When will you reach this goal?

▶ What time limit can you put on this goal?

▶ Habits take 3–4 weeks to form. How long do you need to work at your goal for?

_____

_____

_____

_____

_____

_____

_____

Read through your goal again. Does it fully meet the criteria of a SMART goal? Working towards this goal provides you with a framework to consolidate your progress. Before moving on, check that you are happy with it.

For future use, here is a blank worksheet that you can photocopy.

GOAL WORKSHEET

As of today, I am building the confidence to:

_____

_____

_____

Specific steps: What exactly are you going to achieve?

► What exactly will you have the confidence to do?

► Where will the goal be achieved? (In work? At home? In several locations?)

► Who else, if anyone, does the goal involve?

_____

_____

_____

_____

_____

_____

_____

_____

Measurable outcomes: How will you know when you have reached the goal?

▶ What will you see or hear when you have achieved your goal?

▶ What quantity or numbers can you put on the outcome?

▶ What specific bad feelings will go away? What good feelings will you feel?

_____

_____

_____

_____

_____

_____

_____

Relevant: How is this goal significant to you?

▶ Why is it important to you?

▶ What would it mean if you didn't achieve the goal?

▶ What would it mean if you did achieve the goal?

_____

_____

_____

_____

_____

_____

_____

_____

Time-based: When will you reach this goal?

▶ What time limit can you put on this goal?

▶ Habits take 3–4 weeks to form. How long do you need to work at your goal for?

_____

_____

_____

_____

_____

_____

_____

_____

Congratulations! Just by writing down your goal, you are part of a group who *do things differently.* This is not an easy step. Do you feel different? Probably not. Have you taken the time to congratulate yourself? You *really* should.

Now, do one of the following:

→ Photocopy your filled-out goal worksheet and stick several copies of it up around the house.

→ Type up the goal worksheet (and your answers) on a computer, following the format as above, and print it out; again stick several copies of it up around the house.

You might be tempted to reject this important step, thinking, '*I'll do that at some other point*'. It might even make you feel nervous; you may not believe that you can succeed. And yet, this simple act of making your goals visible will dramatically increase your chances of success. It shows you mean business.

Where to next?

By setting yourself a confidence goal to work towards, you now have a focus for the skills, techniques and abilities acquired through this workbook. There will be challenges along the way, and it is your job now to overcome those challenges – learning as you go.

Throughout this workbook you have been encouraged to put yourself in activating situations to challenge your confidence. As a result you are now gaining the skills you need to be more confident in day-to-day life. Perhaps you are not fully there yet, but you are well on your way.

Your confidence goal provides a framework to work within. There will be specific tasks to achieve, habits to acquire, difficult situations to master and progress to make. The next step is to work out precisely what is required. To do that, you need *an action plan*...

Be more confident

→What have I learnt from this chapter?

▶_____

_____

_____

▶_____

_____

_____

▶_____

_____

_____

→When can I practise these exercises?

▶_____

_____

_____

▶_____

_____

_____

▶_____

_____

_____

12 *Your action plan*

. . . .

In this chapter:
▶ *You will discover how to put your confidence goal into action.*
▶ *You will learn how to create a solid action plan, and how that will help you progress.*
▶ *You will be introduced to a new way of thinking about the time you actually have, and how you plan to use it!*

. . . .

In the previous chapter you set yourself a *confidence goal*, printing out several copies and pinning them up around the house. This goal will be achieved by your thought, persistence and *action*. Goals without action are just empty words. Nothing is more destructive.

Did you set your confidence goal? If not, complete the exercises in the previous chapter. The following exercises will make little sense otherwise.

To achieve your confidence goal you need to act: building skills, establishing habits, ticking boxes and gaining experience. Your goal will not be achieved overnight. Success is arrived at by acting consistently over a period of time.

Imagine a boxer training for the fight of his life. He can't just spend one long day in the gym, lift some weights, perhaps a bit of sparring... *'There, I'm done. Time to put my feet up!'* He will need to train hard for weeks and weeks. Only then will he build the skill, strength and toughness required to succeed. Success is arrived at via action – and nothing else.

Achieving your confidence goal is *your* big fight. As you strive to achieve your goal, you will come up against resistance – especially resistance from yourself. You will ask yourself the question, *do I want to quit?* Your answer to this question will determine your success. In this chapter we will:

▶ Identify all of the actions you could take towards your confidence goal.

▶ Flesh out those actions to form an action plan.

To get anywhere in life, you need to know a) where you're going, and b) how to get there. So, to boost your confidence and achieve your confidence goal, what steps do you need to take?

→ Identifying potential positive action

Take a look at your confidence goal now. To achieve this goal, what skills do you need to develop? What habits do you need to form? What steps do you need to take?

You defined your goal by making it *specific* and *measurable*, so you already have some idea. How can you break it down into small and simple steps? Let's brainstorm the potential positive action you can take. Getting together a comprehensive list is a good place to start.

CASE STUDY – RYAN

Ryan, a 20-year-old student, wants the confidence to get the most from his time at university. His lack of confidence means he shies away from many aspects of university life. Ryan defined his goal as '*building the confidence to push myself at university*'. His goal included specific steps such as asking more questions in lectures, studying more with friends, and spending more time in the library.

Ryan thought of all of the positive actions he could take that would help with his goal:

Start essays earlier   Start going to the gym again   Stop comparing myself to others

Go to the library more   Stop beating myself up for the average marks last year

Ask questions in every lecture   Speak to the brighter students more

CONFIDENCE TO PUSH MYSELF
AT UNIVERSITY

Read course textbooks for an hour every day   Study with Matt and Gemma regularly

Talk to my family about the course when they ask (and when they don't!)

Organize my workspace!   Get back into my hobby – I felt more confident when I was doing it

Learn two new words everyday   Smile at people more – stop frowning so much!

Reviewing Ryan's list of positive actions, we can see that some relate directly to his goal (e.g. reading more, spending more time with the brighter students), and some relate more to his general personal confidence (e.g. smiling more, getting back into the gym).

If Ryan undertakes each of these steps – regularly where required – his confidence levels will improve and he will earn a better degree. Simple cause and effect, as we'll see.

Now it's your turn. Following Ryan's example, be creative and gather together a list of positive actions that will take you towards your goal.

Exercise 38

BRAINSTORMING POTENTIAL POSITIVE ACTION

▶ This exercise takes 10–15 minutes.

▶ The aim is to come up with a rough list of possible actions that will take you towards your goal.

1 Start with a blank sheet of paper; summarize your confidence goal somewhere in the middle.

2 Think about the measurable outcomes you are trying to achieve (refer to your confidence goal worksheet to remind you).

3 Now, scribble down as many potential positive actions you can think of, actions that will contribute – directly or indirectly – towards your goal:

→ **Tasks.** Goals require boxes to be ticked. What smaller steps can you take to achieve your goal?

→ **Habits.** Some goals require repeated actions – what habits do you need to build? *What bad habits do you need to stop?*

→ **Practice.** Everything is practice, including confidence. What could you do to practise being more confident?

→ If your confidence goal involves other people, what opportunities could you make in your life to practise being confident around people generally?

→ If your confidence goal involves taking confident action, what opportunities do you have to practise?

→ **Skills.** What skills do you need to achieve your goal? What actions could you take to develop those skills?

4 Let your pen run free and scribble things down quickly. Don't censor your ideas or put them into order – you will sort through them later.

5 Be as comprehensive as possible – get every action down, no matter how small or obvious.

Spend a good 10–15 minutes on it and write down every relevant action possible. When finished, have a break for 30 minutes or so.

Welcome back. Do you have your sheet full of scribbled ideas? Review the list now – are there any glaring omissions? We want this list to be comprehensive. Keep these notes safe, as you will refer to them often in the coming weeks.

How does this list make you feel – confident or anxious? Remember, you will be taking small steps at first, gaining confidence in your own time. You will decide where to start later in this chapter. For now, let's look at your motivation for change.

→ Why bother now?

To get the most out of this workbook you have been encouraged to *act*. If you want to further increase your confidence, you will need to do 'the work'. This is the reality. Anything else is just kidding yourself.

There are consequences to each and every action we take. For example, when you avoid doing something positive because you lack confidence, several things then happen:

1 You miss out on opportunities in life.

2 However, you avoid the stress of stepping out of your comfort zone.

3 Unfortunately, you also reinforce your lack of confidence, making future avoidance more likely.

4 You will continue to be frustrated by your lack of confidence and progress.

All of our actions have consequences. Whether you achieve your goal or not, there will be consequences to your actions. Let's look at those consequences now.

Exercise 39

SEEING THE CONSEQUENCES

▶ This exercise takes 5–10 minutes.

▶ The aim of this exercise is to fully comprehend the cause of our actions.

1 Think about the consequences of *not* achieving your confidence goal. What will you gain, and what will you lose? What will be different? Write your answers down in the first box below.

2 Then, think about the consequences of achieving your confidence goal. What will you gain? What will you lose? What will be different, better, or worse? Write your answers down in the second box below.

Failing to achieve my confidence goal will result in the following:

→

→

→

→

→

Achieving my confidence goal will result in the following:

→

→

→

→

→

Reflect on your answers a moment. What do you want in life? Do you want your fears to limit you, or do you want to overcome them? Do you want to start now, or do you feel there is plenty of time?

Exercise 40

HOW MUCH TIME DO YOU REALLY HAVE?

▶ This exercise takes 5 minutes.

▶ The aim of this exercise is to demonstrate how limited our time really is.

1 Draw a large circle on a blank sheet of paper. Divide it into half, then quarters, and then eighths.

2 Each section of the circle represents a decade of your life. So, if you're 40, shade in 4 segments, if you're 20 (lucky you!) shade in 2 segments, etc. This represents time that has elapsed so far.

3 We spend a third of our lives asleep, so shade in a third of the remaining segments.

4 How many segments remain? Next, shade in **half** of what is left: *on average a person spends 40 years of their life working or studying, carrying out household chores, looking after the kids, commuting and watching TV!*

5 Take a look: what time is left for you? How much time do you *really* have?

Looking at the time you have left, you may feel anxious, miserable or even depressed. The truth is, we spend a lot of time putting things off. Look again at the consequences of *achieving* your confidence goal versus the consequences of *failing* to achieve it. Which would you rather have in your immediate future?

Then, look at the amount of time you have spent lacking confidence. How much time do you have to build your confidence? What are you *actually* waiting for? You are the only person who can act on your intentions. It is time to complete what you have begun.

SOME THINGS TO REMEMBER

Life is finite and precious. There is so much out there to see, do and experience. An amazing life could be had, providing you find the confidence to have it. The exercises in this book will give you that confidence, so long as you work with them.

Apple founder, Steve Jobs, wrote 'Remembering that I'll be dead soon is the most important tool that I've ever encountered to help me make the big choices in life. Because almost everything just falls away in the face of death, leaving only what is truly important'. There is great truth in this.

Palliative care nurse, Bronnie Ware, spent many years caring for the terminally ill. She writes, 'When people realize that their life is almost over, it is easy to see how many dreams have gone unfulfilled. Most people had not honoured even half of their dreams and had to die knowing that it was due to choices they had made, or not made'.

In life, every action – or inaction – counts towards the quality of your experience; it's what you do that counts. Based on this principle of cause-and-effect, you can achieve your goal and your confidence will continue to improve. Anything else is just an old pattern of negative thinking – a pattern you are seeking to transcend.

Exercise 41

ENVISAGING A CONFIDENT FUTURE

▶ This exercise takes just a couple of minutes.

▶ The aim of this exercise is to think confidently about your future possibilities.

1 In a moment, close your eyes and think about achieving your confidence goal:

  ▷ **Think about how you'd look when you achieve your goal: what you'd be doing, where you'd be doing it, who you'd be doing it with.**

  ▷ **Think about how you'd sound and what you'd say.**

  ▷ **Think about how you'd feel.**

2 Spend a minute or so vividly daydreaming about achieving your goal. Let yourself drift into it, and feel some of the confidence and achievement you would experience. Close your eyes, and try that now.

3 Good. Now, realize that the only thing that stands in between you and that sense of achievement is practice. Get an *action plan* together and follow it through, and your life will change for the better.

Can you see the benefit of taking action? How did it feel to imagine achieving your goal? Now is the time to act. So, let's get a solid plan together.

→ Creating an action plan

Which is more likely to happen: the vague or the specific?

Research shows that knowing *when*, *where* and *how* you want to do something boosts focus and motivation. By adding detail, your list of possible actions becomes a plan.

CASE STUDY – JANICE

Janice, a 50-year-old solicitor, wants the confidence to join an exercise class with her friend. The thought terrifies her; she feels very overweight and has always worried about being clumsy. Here is some of Janice's action plan.

Janice's action plan (example)

What?	How exactly?	Where?	Why?	When?
Buy gym gear.	Shop online (avoid the high street).	At home with my laptop.	I definitely won't go without the right clothing.	Today.
Use an exercise DVD.	I have the one I bought last year. I'll exercise in the spare room.	There is the TV upstairs.	If I can get used to exercising, at least I'll get a feel for it.	When the gym gear arrives.
Speak to Andrea about the Zumba class.	I'll ask about times, cost, etc. I'll make it clear that I'm not going – just asking!	In the office.	It will feel more real if I've spoken to somebody else about it.	Wednesday.

We can see from Janice's plan that she has:

▶ Started small.

▶ Defined realistic actions.

▶ Explained why each action is important.

A good action plan spells things out. Focus and momentum are lost when things aren't clear. It only takes a few minutes to *flesh out* the steps you need to take. By doing so, you make them more likely to happen.

Exercise 42

CREATING YOUR ACTION PLAN

▶ This exercise takes around 5–10 minutes.

▶ The aim is to have a list of clearly defined steps to follow.

1 Previously, you brainstormed a list of actions that will help you towards your goal. Review that list now. Where is the best place to start? Pick three actions that you can do today or tomorrow, and write them in the '*what*' box. Note: choose at least one action that you will find moderately challenging (it can relate directly or indirectly to your goal).

2 If you had to explain these actions to somebody who'd never done anything like it before, what would you say? Write that down in the '*how exactly*' column. Keep it simple.

3 Where do you need to be to carry out the step? Note that down in the '*where*' column.

4 Understanding what you are trying to achieve with the action is important; it provides focus and motivation. Make a note in the *'why'* column.

5 When are you going to take action? Give yourself a target – a deadline; note it down in the *'when'* column. A deadline will also create focus and motivation.

Date:_____

What?	How exactly?	Where?	Why?	When?

Here is a blank table for you to photocopy and use in the future:

Date:_____

What?	How exactly?	Where?	Why?	When?

Well done! You've got three actions to aim for. Now, as before, this plan needs to be visible. Close the book on your plan and you send yourself a powerful, negative message. Instead, do one of the following:

▶ Photocopy today's action plan and stick several copies of it up around the house.

▶ Type up the action plan on a computer, following the format above. Print out several copies and display them next to your confidence goal worksheets, dotted around the house.

Again, you might be tempted to reject this step, thinking, '*I don't need to do this bit*'. However, making your action plan visible will make a tremendous difference.

Where to next?

By getting an action plan together you now know the steps you need to take for greater confidence. If you complete this process every day, your success is virtually guaranteed – providing you actually take the steps! Are you committed to change? Re-read the exercise *'how much time do you really have'* and think about the future.

In the next chapter we will turn our attention to achieving your action plan, and beyond; we will tie up loose ends, and focus firmly on your confident future.

Be more confident

→ What have I learnt from this chapter?

▶ _____

_____

_____

▶ _____

_____

_____

▶ _____

_____

_____

→ When can I practise these exercises?

▶ _____

_____

_____

▶ _____

_____

_____

▶ _____

_____

_____

13 *A confident future*

In this chapter:
- ▶ *You will review your progress so far, and tie up any loose ends.*
- ▶ *You will learn about the importance of resilience, and how to bounce back from setbacks.*
- ▶ *You will discover the real secret of a confident life – and how to harness it for your future success!*

Throughout this workbook, you have been asked to practise a variety of techniques. Some you will have found easy, and others difficult. Some will have made a profound difference, whereas some techniques will have made no difference at all! That is to be expected: confidence differs from person to person.

Before we tie the techniques in this workbook together, let's gauge your progress so far. Answer the following questionnaire. Be honest – this exercise will highlight areas for further improvement.

Self-awareness:

► I have become much more aware of activating situations that damage my confidence:
Not at all: ❑   A little: ❑   A moderate amount: ❑   Significantly: ❑

► I have become much more aware of my thoughts, feelings and behaviours when I lack confidence:
Not at all: ❑   A little: ❑   A moderate amount: ❑   Significantly: ❑

Changing my thinking:

► I can now replace my 'inner critic' with 'my confident inner voice' when I need to:
Not at all: ❑   A little: ❑   A moderate amount: ❑   Significantly: ❑

► I have improved my ability to identify and challenge distorted thinking when it crops up:
Not at all: ❑   A little: ❑   A moderate amount: ❑   Significantly: ❑

► I now have the ability to replace negative mental images with confident imagery:
Not at all: ❑   A little: ❑   A moderate amount: ❑   Significantly: ❑

Overcoming anxiety:

► I now use the 'quick relax' exercise regularly, particularly when I need it:
Not at all: ❑   A little: ❑   A moderate amount: ❑   Significantly: ❑

► I use the 'progressive muscular relaxation' exercise daily, or at least several times per week:
Not at all: ❑   A little: ❑   A moderate amount: ❑   Significantly: ❑

► I have incorporated a relaxing activity into my typical week:
Not at all: ❑   A little: ❑   A moderate amount: ❑   Significantly: ❑

► I notice inflexible thinking quickly, and find it easy to change:
Not at all: ❑   A little: ❑   A moderate amount: ❑   Significantly: ❑

► I notice pessimistic thinking easily, and change it when it crops up:
Not at all: ❑   A little: ❑   A moderate amount: ❑   Significantly: ❑

Feeling more confident:

► I can now use the 'spinning feelings' technique to reduce negative feelings:
Not at all: ❑   A little: ❑   A moderate amount: ❑   Significantly: ❑

► I can now use the 'spinning feelings' technique to increase confident feelings at will:
Not at all: ❑   A little: ❑   A moderate amount: ❑   Significantly: ❑

Taking confident action:

▶ **I am good at identifying procrastination when I find myself doing it:**
Not at all: ❑   A little: ❑   A moderate amount: ❑   Significantly: ❑

▶ **I can recognize – and dismiss – procrastination excuses easily:**
Not at all: ❑   A little: ❑   A moderate amount: ❑   Significantly: ❑

▶ **I have practised the exercise to build motivation and find it much easier to get started:**
Not at all: ❑   A little: ❑   A moderate amount: ❑   Significantly: ❑

Freedom from the past:

▶ **I have identified damaging negative experiences from my past and desensitized them:**
Not at all: ❑   A little: ❑   A moderate amount: ❑   Significantly: ❑

▶ **I have identified and changed limiting negative beliefs:**
Not at all: ❑   A little: ❑   A moderate amount: ❑   Significantly: ❑

Interpersonal confidence:

I have successfully used the exercise to socialize confidently:
Not at all: ❑   A little: ❑   A moderate amount: ❑   Significantly: ❑

▶ **I have successfully used the exercise to view myself through the eyes of a loved one:**
Not at all: ❑   A little: ❑   A moderate amount: ❑   Significantly: ❑

▶ **I am skilled at challenging negative thoughts when they crop up in social situations:**
Not at all: ❑   A little: ❑   A moderate amount: ❑   Significantly: ❑

Safety behaviours:

▶ **I have identified, and changed, safety behaviours – including safety behaviours in social situations:**
Not at all: ❑   A little: ❑   A moderate amount: ❑   Significantly: ❑

Goal-setting:

▶ **I have set a SMART confidence goal:**
Not at all: ❑   A little: ❑   A moderate amount: ❑   Significantly: ❑

▶ **I have designed an action plan for my confidence goal:**
Not at all: ❑   A little: ❑   A moderate amount: ❑   Significantly: ❑

Review your answers. Where have you done well, and what can you improve? Where your answers are 'not at all' or 'a little', re-read the relevant chapter and practise with the exercises. The techniques in this workbook are not difficult, but they do require some persistence.

Think about a 'typical' confident person. On a day-to-day basis, they will:

▶ Think confidently in most situations.

▶ Be generally optimistic about life.

▶ Rarely become anxious about their performance.

▶ Typically feel confident and in control.

▶ Take confident action, with little procrastination.

▶ Communicate confidently with others, feeling at ease and free of fidgeting, discomfort and self-consciousness.

▶ Be free of limiting beliefs.

▶ Find safety behaviour unnecessary.

▶ Have an idea of what they want from life, and an understanding of how to get it.

If you answered *a moderate amount* or *significantly* to many of the questions above, then you are well on your way to being confident. It is useful to bear in mind this quote from author and philosopher Will Durant:

Excellence is an art won by training and habituation: we do not act rightly because we have virtue or excellence, but we rather have these because we have acted rightly; 'these virtues are formed in man by his doing the actions'; we are what we repeatedly do. Excellence, then, is not an act but a habit.

Replace the word *excellence* with *confidence*, and you have the secret to a confident life. Habitually use the techniques you have learnt, and your confidence will be evident to all, including the toughest judge of your character – yourself.

There is one more thing a 'typical' confident person will do. They will:

▶ Act each day to get what they want in life.

Before we move on, do you need to re-read any chapters above?

→ Confidence means action

In the previous chapter, you came up with an action plan – a *road map* to your confidence goal. Implement this action plan fully, and you will achieve your goal and continue to grow in confidence. Then, choose a second goal, devise a new action plan, and achieve that goal as well. Confidence is found in the *achievement* of these goals. Understand that truth, and you are well on your way.

On completion of your second goal, simply choose a third. After all, what use is confidence if you are not going to *use* it?

▶ Achieve your confidence goal(s), and your life becomes more enjoyable.

▶ Acting towards your goals gives you opportunities to use your new skills.

In a way, it is simple: implement each step of your action plan(s), and your success in life is virtually guaranteed. Providing you keep going, there is no failure. You might not be used to thinking this way, *but understanding this rational, fundamental truth is the final step to life-changing confidence.*

Confident people might change course, but they never give up. Combine this truth with the Will Durant quote above, and you have everything you need to be a success in life. All you need now is a bit of resilience.

→ Personal resilience

Bouncing back from setbacks takes resilience. As you work towards your confidence goal(s), things are bound to go wrong occasionally:

▶ Even with the best laid plans, life will sometimes get in the way.

▶ As you grow in confidence, the odd difficult experience will just come out of the blue.

▶ Not every day will be your 'personal best'; sometimes you'll take your foot off the pedal.

▶ And as you become more confident, some people might try and drag you down.

Confident people go through their difficult patches too; the difference is in their *response*. Instead of feeling defeated, confident people dust themselves off and carry on. Resilience transforms failure into temporary disappointment.

Exercise 43

BOUNCING BACK FROM SETBACKS

▶ This exercise takes around 10 minutes.

▶ The aim is to change the way you feel about setbacks so they do not bring you down.

▶ Use it a day or two after a difficult experience – in time, resilience will come naturally.

Part 1 – desensitization

To begin, let's take the sting out of the setback. For most situations, the rewind technique is ideal.

1 In a moment, close your eyes, and recall the experience that knocked you back. See what you saw, hear what you heard and feel what you felt. Try that now, and make a note of your feelings in the space below (direction of feeling refers to the way the feeling moves through your body – see Chapter 5 for more information):

Type of feeling: _____

Strength of feeling: _____

Location in body: _____

Direction of feeling: _____

2 Then, visualize the experience again. This time – place it on a small black-and-white screen in your mind's eye, and view it in the third person, so you see yourself in the picture.

3 Play the visualization forwards in your mind, from the beginning to the end. If you need to, summarize the difficult experience into a 10-second clip, so that you get the gist of what happened.

4 Then, rewind the visualization; play it backwards in your mind, from the end to the beginning. Take your time, and work out how it looks as it plays forwards and backwards. Pay attention to the order in which events unfold, etc. Aim to keep it small, black-and-white, third person, and on a screen – as if watching it on a CCTV camera in your mind.

5 When you have the hang of it, play the visualization forwards and backwards five times. Then, open and close your eyes, and play it again five more times. Repeat this process until it looks and feels like it is happening to somebody else, as if you were watching TV.

It will be difficult to keep the mental image small and black-and-white at first, but soon it will become easier. After just 5–10 minutes, you'll find yourself unable to feel anything negative about the experience. It will just feel like an old memory.

You will be familiar with the rewind technique from Chapter 7; you can read a comprehensive description of the exercise there. Compared to working with difficult childhood memories, the desensitization effect will occur quickly. Aim to get over the tricky first couple of minutes, and the rest will be straightforward.

Part 2 – building determination to bounce back

The second part of the exercise associates your next task (on your action plan) with positive, motivated feelings.

1 Stop for a moment – how does it feel when you feel really confident? Imagine bouncing back from your setback with even more determination. In a moment, close your eyes and feel determined to carry on (it is okay if you have to force it a little – that is normal for most people).

2 Try that now, and make a note of your feelings in the space below:

Type of feeling: _____

Strength of feeling: _____

Location in body: _____

Direction of feeling: _____

3 Now, using the 'spinning feelings' technique from Chapter 5, close your eyes and imagine the scene again. This time, spin this determined feeling around your body so it becomes faster, vibrant, and more powerful...

4 As you spin this feeling around, imagine carrying out the tasks you have planned for today. It is important to imagine the detail involved. Keep the determined feelings spinning around as you do this.

5 Continue picturing the detail of your next tasks and spinning determined feelings around your body. Tell yourself, using your confident voice, *'Avoiding these tasks is pointless – I will bounce back today!'*

6 Then, open your eyes and realize: *you can do anything you want – you just need to start*. Ideally, start one of your tasks straight away.

Remember: confident people also experience difficulty – the difference is in their response. Use this technique frequently enough, and you too will acquire the habit of bouncing back.

→ A positive relationship with yourself

Despite increased confidence in day-to-day life, some people will feel that their confidence is just a façade. If you experience such thoughts, the exercises in Chapters 7 and 8 will help. Ask yourself: what negative belief is holding me back? Is there a part of me still stuck in the past? Use the rewind technique and the belief change exercise on any memory that makes you feel bad about yourself, and you will free yourself of such thinking.

Even without using that process, you can realize that you are not your beliefs. If you feel inferior to others (or that you will be rejected by others) – work to change such beliefs immediately.

You do not need to be popular, beautiful, or a genius to have real confidence. If you are overweight or feel shy around others (or whatever weakness you still focus on), accepting the reality of who you are is a good first step. None of us are perfect; there are always challenges, even if some are lucky enough to be dealt an easy hand.

From there, remember that we are rarely stuck with our weaknesses. If you genuinely feel held back by some aspect of your *self*, you now have the goal-setting tools and techniques required to create change in your life. Most things can be improved with focus, resilience and practice.

So, if there are practical steps you can undertake to change your limitations – those aspects of yourself you wish you could change – then prioritize those steps. In the meantime, this following exercise will help.

Exercise 44

ACCEPTING YOUR GOOD POINTS

▶ This exercise takes 5 minutes.

▶ The aim is to understand (and accept) that other people view you differently.

1 Ask a (trusted) friend to write down five things they like, respect, or love about you. Do the same in return.

2 When you get the list – accept the reality of it. Other people's views of us often contain a clarity we struggle to achieve ourselves.

3 Keep the list safe, and refer to it once per day for the next month or so.

A simple exercise, then. The thought of it might leave you feeling anxious, which would be telling in itself. If so, do not skip this exercise – it is important to see yourself in a new light.

→ Preparing for success

Nothing bolsters confidence more than success. Take a look at your action plan, and review the three actions you can carry out today. Let's focus on taking those steps right now.

Exercise 45

TAKE ACTION!

▶ This exercise takes 10 minutes or so to write up.

▶ The aim is to make progress towards your confidence goal, ideally using your new skills.

Focus on this process daily (take a day off at weekends) and turn it into a habit. Goal-oriented people are the most successful in life.

1 What are your three tasks for today? Now is the time to make a start on them. Can you think of an excuse not to? If so, use the exercises from Chapter 6 to dismiss any excuses. It is time to make a start.

2 Use your new skills: if you need to change negative thoughts as they crop up, then change them. If you need to ease past anxiety and build confident feelings in your body, then do so. If you need to overcome safety behaviour, use the techniques that will help, and so on.

Remember that you will not be perfectly confident. You will not perfectly change your thoughts or feelings. However, by practising several times daily, your confidence is guaranteed to improve.

Refer to the checklist at the beginning of this chapter. Ideally, practise the skills you have not yet mastered.

3 Make a start on the tasks. When complete, use the ABC sheets below to record your experience.

Writing down your results accelerates learning and significantly contributes towards your growing confidence. As you work towards your first confidence goal, use the ABC records each time you act. When you progress to the second confidence goal (and beyond), use the ABC records only to record something noteworthy, e.g. an unexpected challenge or a particularly positive experience.

4 Finally, create a new action plan for tomorrow. With your list of brainstormed actions to hand, complete the *creating your action plan* exercise once more (see Chapter 12) in the space below. Defining tomorrow's steps today is a *very* helpful habit – do not skip this step!

5 Repeat steps 1 – 3 each day until you have achieved your confidence goal.

Some points to remember:

▶ It might take a week, or a month, or even longer, but you will get there if you act frequently.

▶ Sometimes we need to take the *same step several times* until successful; we cannot get everything right first time.

▶ Take one day off from your action plan each week.

▶ Each week, when you have achieved 80 per cent of your tasks, allow yourself one significant and enjoyable treat. When it comes – savour it.

▶ Remember – keep going and your success is virtually guaranteed. Learning to bounce back from setbacks is key. The exercise earlier in this chapter will help.

In an ideal world, you will complete three tasks each day. Each task you carry out will contribute towards greater personal and interpersonal confidence – sometimes directly, and sometimes indirectly. Anticipate some difficult experiences, and aim to give your new skills time to flourish.

Consider your answers to the questionnaire at the start of this chapter. Where possible, focus on your weaknesses and improve them. If your problems are mostly with interpersonal confidence, prioritize social activities. Difficulties with performance anxiety? Master the techniques in Chapter 4 until you've cracked it.

Focusing on tasks that improve your weaknesses is a good strategy, whereas avoiding your weaknesses is a subtle form of *safety behaviour* and should be avoided.

THE ABC OF IMPROVING CONFIDENCE.

Use these three ABC tables to record your experiences as you carry out today's action plan. Then, use the table below to create a new action plan for tomorrow, following the exercise from the previous chapter (*creating your action plan*).

My ABC tables and action plan

Activating situation:	
Belief:	
Consequences:	
Helpful techniques used:	

Activating situation:	
Belief:	
Consequences:	
Helpful techniques used:	

Activating situation:	
Belief:	
Consequences:	
Helpful techniques used:	

Tomorrow's action plan:

Date:_____

What?	How exactly?	Where?	Why?	When?

Here are some blank sheets for you to photocopy.

My ABC tables and action plan

Activating situation:	
Belief:	
Consequences:	
Helpful techniques used:	

Activating situation:	
Belief:	
Consequences:	
Helpful techniques used:	

Activating situation:	
Belief:	
Consequences:	
Helpful techniques used:	

Tomorrow's action plan:

Date:_____

What?	How exactly?	Where?	Why?	When?

Above all, remember that your efforts will not be perfect. Instead, look to practise, learn and grow in confidence *gradually*. Occasionally, things will go wrong. Put it down to experience, and keep going – your confident life is waiting for you.

Where to next?

Throughout this workbook, confidence has been defined in many different ways. Without confidence, people struggle with limitation, frustration and even fear. Confidence is freedom – the freedom to be who you want to be.

People do not wake up one morning and think, '*I have confidence!*' It is not a medal to be worn proudly. Instead, confidence is a process that flows through time, rising and falling as we go through life. Although people talk of having more confidence, or of being more confident around others, confidence is truly reflected in the life we choose to live and share with others.

With confidence comes a certainty *that your efforts will be rewarded*. You will not be successful in everything you try – we all experience defeat and disappointment. But confidence allows you to bounce back, turning your dreams of a better future into reality.

In Chapter 2, you highlighted areas in your life where you want more confidence. You now have the necessary tools to transform your desire into *action*. Focus on those areas, define (and achieve) your goals, and your confidence will become evident in *everything you do*. Stick to your plan, and one month from now things will have noticeably improved.

Keep going and, three to six months from now, your life will be virtually unrecognizable. That progress exists only in the steps you take each day, starting with today. Good luck, and be bold.

Be more confident

→ What have I learnt from this chapter?

▶ _____

_____

_____

▶ _____

_____

_____

▶ _____

_____

_____

→ When can I practise these exercises?

▶ _____

_____

_____

▶ _____

_____

_____

▶ _____

_____

_____

Appendix I

Occasionally in life, we face challenging situations that take us out of our comfort zone. From public speaking and job interviews, to dealing with medical procedures, to attending the first day of an evening course or starting at a new gym – life is full of situations that challenge our confidence.

The following process, if applied thoroughly enough, will help you to feel confident about *anything*.

→ Part I – in advance

PREPARATION

What preparation can you do in advance? Do you need to write a speech? Get some books together? Do you need to watch an instructional video or speak to a professional? In part, confidence comes from competence – you need to prepare thoroughly.

KNOW WHAT THE SITUATION IS

What can you find out about the situation you're entering into? As people, we harbour an irrational fear of the unknown – it wreaks havoc with confidence. As far as you can, know what to expect in advance. This will go *some way* to alleviating fear – at least to an extent.

DESENSITIZE NEGATIVE EXPERIENCES FROM THE PAST

Have you struggled in similar situations in the past? If so, use the rewind technique (Chapter 7) on your memory of the event until it is thoroughly desensitized. This will remove a lot of fear, and your chances of success dramatically increase as a result. When considering which memories to desensitize, consider earlier experiences that are similar in dynamic or context.

For example, if you are worried about a public speaking engagement, check to see if there were difficult experiences (involving scrutiny or being on the spot) at school, university, or in your first job.

OVERCOMING SAFETY BEHAVIOUR

In Chapter 10 you learnt about safety behaviours – the technique in this chapter will help with avoidance, escape and social safety behaviours. Use this technique if you anticipate safety behaviour being a problem.

USE THE BELIEF CHANGE PROCESS

Do you feel certain that it will all go wrong? It is always a good idea to use the belief change exercise beforehand. Use the technique (in Chapter 8) to make the idea of things going wrong seem unbelievable. Then, complete the process so a positive outcome feels more and more believable.

→ Part 2 – on the day

EASE ANXIETY AWAY

On the day itself, aim to combine the 'overcoming safety behaviour' exercise with the relaxation techniques in Chapter 4. It is natural to feel anxious before challenging situations. However, by relaxing, you increase your chances of thinking positively. Even seasoned performers feel anxious before going on stage – the aim is to harness that energy to sharpen your performance, rather than detract from it.

CHANGE NEGATIVE THOUGHTS AS THEY CROP UP

Notice and squash any negative thoughts at this point – habitually, they could crop up. The techniques in Chapter 3 will help if negative thinking is a problem.

REMOVE NEGATIVE FEELINGS / SPIN POSITIVE FEELINGS

Controlling your state of mind is vital just before a challenging situation. This is also true for the first few minutes. Use the techniques to spin feelings – aim to weaken negative feelings (if they crop up), and get good feelings spinning around your body. That energy will carry you through.

PERFORM WITH PASSION

Does the situation involve people? If so, there will be an element of performance involved. So, when it comes to the moment, put some passion and focus into it. Again, this energy will carry you through.

This full process represents a couple of hours' work, which isn't too much effort when you consider what is at stake. Ultimately, your chances of success reflect the effort you put in. To get the most out of this work, it pays to practise with the exercises frequently – using them in day-to-day situations until you feel *confident* in them.

Appendix II

Here are the ABC table, goal worksheet and action plan templates used in this workbook.

ABC table

Activating situation:	
Belief:	
Consequences:	
Techniques Used:	

GOAL WORKSHEET

As of today, I am building the confidence to:

_____

_____

_____

Specific steps: What exactly are you going to achieve?

- ▶ What exactly will you have the confidence to do?

- ▶ Where will the goal be achieved? (In work? At home? In several locations?)

- ▶ Who else, if anyone, does the goal involve?

_____

_____

_____

_____

_____

_____

_____

Measurable outcomes: How will you know when you have reached the goal?

- ▶ What will you see or hear when you have achieved your goal?

► What quantity or numbers can you put on the outcome?

► What specific bad feelings will go away? What good feelings will you feel?

_____

_____

_____

_____

_____

_____

_____

_____

Relevant: How is this goal significant to you?

► Why is it important to you?

► What would it mean if you didn't achieve the goal?

► What would it mean if you did achieve the goal?

_____

_____

_____

_____

_____

_____

_____

_____

Time-based: When will you reach this goal?

▶ What time limit can you put on this goal?

▶ Habits take 3–4 weeks to form. How long do you need to work at your goal for?

_____

_____

_____

_____

_____

Tomorrow's action plan:

Date:_____

What?	How exactly?	Where?	Why?	When?

Index